# Communications
# in Computer and Information Science 1300

More information about this series at http://www.springer.com/series/7899

Feng Tian · Xiaosong Yang ·
Daniel Thalmann · Weiwei Xu ·
Jian Jun Zhang · Nadia Magnenat Thalmann ·
Jian Chang (Eds.)

# Computer Animation and Social Agents

33rd International Conference
on Computer Animation and Social Agents, CASA 2020
Bournemouth, UK, October 13–15, 2020
Proceedings

 Springer

*Editors*
Feng Tian
Faculty of Science and Technology
Bournemouth University
Poole, UK

Daniel Thalmann
École Polytechnique Fédérale de Lausa
Lausanne, Switzerland

Jian Jun Zhang
Faculty of Media and Communication
Bournemouth University
Poole, UK

Jian Chang ⓘ
Faculty of Media and Communication
Bournemouth University
Poole, UK

Xiaosong Yang
Faculty of Media and Communication
Bournemouth University
Poole, UK

Weiwei Xu
Computer Science Department
Zhejiang University
Hangzhou, China

Nadia Magnenat Thalmann ⓘ
MIRALab/C.U.I.
University of Geneva
Geneva, Switzerland

ISSN 1865-0929            ISSN 1865-0937 (electronic)
Communications in Computer and Information Science
ISBN 978-3-030-63425-4       ISBN 978-3-030-63426-1 (eBook)
https://doi.org/10.1007/978-3-030-63426-1

This Springer imprint is published by the registered company Springer Nature Switzerland AG
The registered company address is: Gewerbestrasse 11, 6330 Cham, Switzerland

# Preface

Welcome to the 33rd International Conference on Computer Animation and Social Agents (CASA 2020). Due to COVID-19 the conference was held online during October 13–15, 2020. The conference is organized by Bournemouth University, UK, together with the Computer Graphics Society (CGS).

CASA is the oldest international conference in computer animation and social agents in the world. Since it was founded in Geneva, Switzerland, in 1988 under the name of Computer Animation (CA), CASA become an international forum for researchers and practitioners to present their latest research in Computer Animation, Embodied Agents, Social Agents, Virtual and Augmented Reality, and Visualization. In the past decade, CASA was held in Belgium (2007), South Korea (2008), The Netherlands (2009), France (2010), China (2011), Singapore (2012), Turkey (2013), the USA (2014), Singapore (2015), Switzerland (2016), South Korea (2017), China (2018) and France (2019).

Included in this volume of conference proceedings, we have contributions from academics, which aim to advance technologies and address challenging issues in all fields related to computer animation and social agent, ranging from animation, modeling, and visualization to image processing, virtual reality, etc. There are 86 submissions to CASA 2020, and each of which has been reviewed by three reviewers of our International Program Committee. 42 papers were accepted for the journal *Computer Animation and Social Agents*, and 14 papers for this volume.

We would like to thank all members of the International Program Committee for their devotion to the conference in the past years, and their expert reviews for the papers, which have provided valuable feedback to the authors. Finally, we would like to thank Bournemouth University for hosting and organizing the conference.

September 2020

Feng Tian
Xiaosong Yang
Daniel Thalmann
Weiwei Xu
Jian Jun Zhang
Nadia Magnenat Thalmann
Jian Chang

# Organization

## Conference Co-chairs

Jian Jun Zhang          Bournemouth University, UK
Nadia Magnenat Thalmann    University of Geneva, Switzerland, and Nanyang
                                   Technological University, Singapore

## Program Co-chairs

Daniel Thalmann       EPFL, Switzerland
Xiaosong Yang         Bournemouth University, UK
Weiwei Xu             Zhejiang University, China

## Publicity Chair

Jian Chang           Bournemouth University, UK

## Local Chair

Feng Tian             Bournemouth University, UK

## International Program Committee

Nadine Aburumman     Brunel University London, UK
Norman Badler         University of Pennsylvania, USA
Selim Balcisoy         Sabanci University, Turkey
Loic Barthe           IRIT, Université de Toulouse, France
Jan Bender            RWTH Aachen University, Germany
Raphaëlle Chaine      LIRIS, Université Lyon 1, France
Jian Chang           Bournemouth University, UK
Fred Charles          Bournemouth University, UK
Parag Chaudhuri       IIT Bombay, India
Marc Christie          Inria, France
Justin Dauwels        Nanyang Technological University, Singapore
Shujie Deng          King's College London, UK
Zhigang Deng         University of Houston, USA
Christos Gatzidis      Bournemouth University, UK
Ugur Gudukbay       Bilkent University, Turkey
Shihui Guo           Xiamen University, China
Xiaohu Guo          The University of Texas at Dallas, USA
James Hahn           George Washington University, USA
Carlo Harvey         Birmingham City University, UK

viii     Organization

| | |
|---|---|
| Ying He | Nanyang Technological University, Singapore |
| Gaoqi He | East China Normal University, China |
| Ruizhen Hu | Shenzhen University, China |
| Jinyuan Jia | Tongji University, China |
| Tao Jiang | University of Surrey, UK |
| Xiaogang Jin | Zhejiang University, China |
| Marcelo Kallmann | University of California, Merced, USA |
| Prem Kalra | IIT Delhi, India |
| Dongwann Kang | Seoul National University of Science and Technology, South Korea |
| Mubbasir Kapadia | Rutgers University, USA |
| Min H. Kim | Korea Advanced Institute of Science and Technology, South Korea |
| Scott King | Texas A&M University, USA |
| Taesoo Kwon | Hanyang University, China |
| Sung-Hee Lee | Korea Advanced Institute of Science and Technology, South Korea |
| Wonsook Lee | University of Ottawa, Canada |
| Tsai-Yen Li | National Chengchi University, Taiwan |
| Guoliang Luo | East China Jiaotong University, China |
| Chongyang Ma | Snap Inc., USA |
| Anderson Maciel | Universidade Federal do Rio Grande do Sul, Brazil |
| Nadia Magnenat Thalmann | University of Geneva, Switzerland |
| Shigeo Morishima | Waseda University, Japan |
| Soraia Musse | Pontificia Universidade Catolica do Roi Grande do Sul, Brazil |
| Rahul Narain | IIT Delhi, India |
| Junjun Pan | Beihang University, China |
| Nuria Pelechano | Universitat Politècnica de Catalunya, Spain |
| Julien Pettre | Inria, France |
| Nicolas Pronost | Université Claude Bernard Lyon 1, France |
| Kun Qian | King's College London, UK |
| Kemao Qian | Nanyang Technological University, Singapore |
| Abdennour El Rhalibi | Liverpool John Moores University, UK |
| Craig Schroeder | University of California, Riverside, USA |
| Ari Shapiro | Embody Digital, USA |
| Hubert P. H. Shum | University of Northumbria, UK |
| Etienne de Sevin | SANPSY, University of Bordeaux, France |
| Shinjiro Sueda | Texas A&M University, USA |
| Daniel Thalmann | Ecole Polytechnique Fédérale de Lausanne, Switzerland |
| Feng Tian | Bournemouth University, UK |
| Yiying Tong | Michigan State University, USA |
| Meili Wang | Northwest A&F University, China |
| Zhao Wang | Zhejiang University, China |
| Enhua Wu | University of Macau and ISCAS, China |

# Contents

# Modelling, Animation and Simulation

# ESENet: A Human Behavior Recognition Model Based on Extended Squeeze-and-Excitation Network

Lei Chen[1], Rui Liu[1(✉)], Dongsheng Zhou[1,2(✉)], Xin Yang[2], Qiang Zhang[1,2], and Xiaopeng Wei[2]

[1] Key Laboratory of Advanced Design and Intelligent Computing (Ministry of Education), School of Software Engineering, Dalian University, Dalian, China
{liurui,zhouds}@dlu.edu.cn
[2] School of Computer Science and Technology, Dalian University of Technology, Dalian, China

**Abstract.** Human behavior recognition in video sequences is an important research problem in computer vision, and has attracted a lot of researchers' attention in recent years. Because of its powerful ability in feature channels recalibration, the Squeeze-and-Excitation network (SE network) has been widely used in video behavior recognition models. However, most of these methods use the SE network directly to recalibrate different feature channels of a single frame image, but ignore the temporal dimension of videos. To address this problem, a new behavior recognition model based on extended Squeeze-and-Excitation network (named as ESENet) is proposed in this study. In order to improve the attention capability, the integration strategy of the 3DSE is also discussed in this study. Experiment results show that the proposed method in this paper achieves competitive performance on the challenging HMDB51, UCF101, and Something-Something v1 datasets.

**Keywords:** Behavior recognition · Extended Squeeze-and-Excitation network · ESENet

## 1 Introduction

As an important branch of the computer vision, video behavior recognition has a wide range of applications in our daily life. However, as the complexity of human behaviors, it is also a challenging task. In recent years, researchers have proposed many approaches to improve the performance of behavior recognition. These methods can be divided into artificial features based approaches and deep learning based approaches. Although these methods have achieved some results, how to make the machine understand the behaviors in videos as accurately and efficiently as humans is still an open problem. Therefore, it is meaningful and valuable to study the characteristics of the human visual system and integrate it into the existing behavior recognition models. According to some studies, when humans observe a video clip, they don't give the same attention to each frame of videos or different spatial parts of videos' frame. Specially, in order to understand the

© Springer Nature Switzerland AG 2020
F. Tian et al. (Eds.): CASA 2020, CCIS 1300, pp. 3–13, 2020.
https://doi.org/10.1007/978-3-030-63426-1_1

behavior in a video, people usually focus on the more important spatial part in a frame or the video frames that contain more discriminative information. This is the human visual attention mechanism. Therefore, adding an attention mechanism module into the behavior recognition model is logical and reasonable for improving the effect of the model.

The Squeeze-and-Excitation network [1] is a commonly used attention mechanism model and widely used in behavior recognition models. However, some methods such as [2] use the SE module directly just like the image classification, in which SE is used to recalibrate the feature channel of a single frame image to enhance the useful feature channels and suppress the useless feature channels. Although these approaches could model the relationship between different feature channels to a certain extent, they don't refer to the temporal information of the entire sequence. This is likely to result in some feature channels being given important weights. However these feature channels are only more important in a certain frame but less important in the entire motion sequence. So this would result in these feature channels being wrongly recalibrated and therefore reduce the final recognition effect. For example, "running" may be more important information in the first few frames of a "pole-vault" action, but the final "pole-vault" movement is the most distinguishing information for the entire video. Therefore, if relationships among feature channels are modeled only taking account into information of a single frame image, a "pole-vault" action may be misidentified as a "run" action.

In order to solve the problem mentioned above, a new behavior recognition model named ESENet is proposed in this study, in which an extended Squeeze-and-Excitation network named 3DSE [3] is introduced into the 3D CNN (3D convolutional neural network) part. Different with previous methods, the input of 3DSE module is not feature maps of a single frame, but feature maps of N frame images. The benefit of this approach is that the wrong feature channel recalibration is avoided to a certain extent, so the recognition accuracy is improved.

## 2   Related Work

Methods of video behavior recognition mainly include traditional methods based on artificial design features and approaches based on the deep learning technology. Among them, the traditional behavior recognition methods, such as IDT [4], template matching [5] et al., have achieved some effects. But there are still some problems, such as poor generalization ability of models and depending heavily on manual experience and knowledge for feature constructing. Therefore, with the wide application of the deep learning technology, the traditional methods have been gradually replaced by the methods based on deep learning. Now, some traditional feature descriptors are often combined with the features extracted by deep learning techniques, such as DTTP + IDT [6].

The behavior recognition methods based on deep learning can be divided into several types as following: two-stream networks [7, 8], 3D convolutional neural network [9, 10] and 2D (2D convolutional neural network), 3D (3D convolutional neural network) hybrid network [11–13]. Among them, the methods based on two-stream network need to spend a lot of time on the temporal stream to calculate the optical flow information, and can't model the complex temporal information effectively. Although the approaches based on

3D CNN can deal with complex temporal sequence information, it also results in some problems. For example, models become more complex and contain large quantities of parameters, which make them not easy to be employed in practical applications. The 2D and 3D hybrid networks make use of 2DCNN to process spatial information, and 3DCNN to model temporal information. The methods reduce the complexity of the models while ensuring the effect of them. Therefore, we also used a 2D and 3D mixed behavior recognition model, ResNet34-3DRes18, as our baseline model in this paper.

With studying and understanding the characteristics of the human visual system, the use of the attention mechanism in some models has become an important issue focused by researchers. Jaderberg et al. [14] proposed a spatial transformer module that makes the network to focus on those spatial regions with more discriminative information. On the basis of the original LRCN [15] network, An et al. [2] added the attention mechanism module SE to recalibrate the feature channels extracted by the spatial feature extraction network, and improved the effect of the original method. Comparing with other attention mechanism models, SE can be easily embedded into existing behavior recognition networks, and the use of SE only adds a small amount of parameters. Therefore, SE is widely used in 2DCNN networks to model the relationships of spatial feature channels such as Res34-SE-IM-Net [16]. But this model only considers the information of a single frame of image, which may make some feature channels to be wrongly recalibrated. Addressing this problem, the 3DSE module which fully made use of multi-frame information to recalibrate feature channels, is used as the attention module, and an improved behavior recognition model, ESENet, is constructed in this paper.

## 3 Methods

### 3.1 ESENet

A 2D and 3D fused behavior recognition model ResNet34-3DRes18, is used as the baseline model in this paper. Based on this, the 3DSE module is added to construct an attention behavior recognition model named ESENet. The network architecture is shown in Fig. 1.

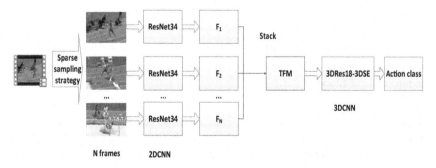

**Fig. 1.** The architecture of ESENet network.

For HMDB51, UCF101 and Something-Something v1 datasets used in our experiments, we analysed that the duration of each clips in these datasets is shorter about 2 s–10 s. Meanwhile, the changes of video segments in short time is smaller, and the adjacent frame images in a video segment are so similar that they are difficult to distinguish. Therefore, we have adopted a sparse sampling strategy [17] to acquire the input of model. Specifically, each video is first divided into N (N = 16, the details in Sect. 4.1) segments of equal length, and one frame of image is randomly sampled from each segment as the input of the 2DCNN part. Then, the input images are processed by 2D CNN part (ResNet34 [18] network up to layer 4), and N feature maps $F_i(1 \leq i \leq N)$(in this $F_i \in R^{512 \times 7 \times 7}$) are obtained. Finally, the N feature maps are stacked into a new feature map, named as TFM (Temporal Feature Map), which is processed by 3D CNN part (3DRes18-3DSE network) to get final action recognition result: Action class.

The 3D CNN part consists of a modified 3DRes18 network and 3DSE module. Specifically, the 3DSE module and the Block in the 3DRes18 network are fused to form a new Block, named 3DSE-Block which replaces the original Block in the 3DRes18 network, as shown in Fig. 2.

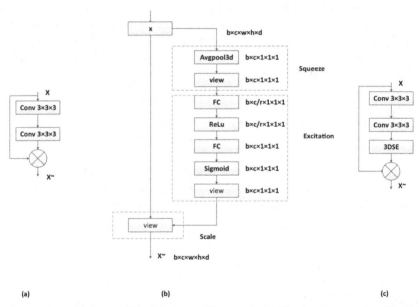

(a)                          (b)                          (c)

**Fig. 2.** (a) The architecture of Block in 3DRes18 network; (b) The architecture of 3DSE; (c) The architecture of 3DSE-Block.

The Fig. 2 (a) shows the specific structure of the Block in the 3DRes18 network, which make up of two 3D convolutional layers with convolutional kernel; The Fig. 2 (b) represents the basic structure of 3DSE module which consists of the Squeeze operation, Excitation operation and Scale operation like SE Module; The Fig. 2(c) shows the structure of 3DSE-Block. In this, the 3DSE is placed after the second 3D convolutional layer of the Block. For a 3DSE-Block, its internal processing of the input is as follows:

$$u^{conv-x} = f_{conv}(f_{conv}(x)) \qquad (1)$$

As shown in Eq. (1), the input $x(x \in R^{b \times c \times w \times h \times d})$ is first processed by two consecutive convolution operations to get $u^{conv-x}$ which is the input of 3DSE module. $f_{conv}$ is a 3D convolution whose kernel size is $3 \times 3 \times 3$, stride is 1, and padding is 1. The represents a feature map got by two consecutive operations. And then, it is processed by 3DSE module, and a new recalibrated feature map $u^{conv-3DSE}$ is got, as shown in Eq. (2).

$$u^{conv-3DSE} = f_{3DSE}(u^{conv-x}) \qquad (2)$$

In the equation, $f_{3DSE}$ represents a 3DSE module which consists of Squeeze, Excitation and Scale operations, as shown in Fig. 2(b). Finally, the original input $x$ and $u^{conv-3DSE}$ are merged by identity mapping, the final output of 3DSE-Block is got, as shown in Eq. 3.

$$x^{\sim} = x + u^{conv-3DSE} \qquad (3)$$

### 3.2 The Integration of 3DSE and 3DCNN

At first, similar with the integration strategy of SE and 2DCNN, we placed the 3DSE module behind the second BN layer in the Block of 3DRes18 network (3DCNN). This structure was named as BN-SE-Block, as shown in Fig. 3 (a). But in the experiments, we found that this structure didn't play a positive role in the network and the results were even worse than before. Through the analysis, the reason may be the wrong position order of the BN layer and 3DSE. Because the main function of the BN layer is to normalize the data obtained by the convolutional layer, which may destroy the information needed by 3DSE. Therefore, we adjusted the location of BN layer and 3DSE module to form a new network structure named as SE-BN-Block, in which the 3DSE module is placed directly after the second convolutional layer in the Block, as shown in Fig. 3(b). The later experiments showed that the SE-BN-Block acquired better performance than the BN-SE-Block on different datasets. Therefore, the SE-BN-Block was used instead of BN-SE-Block in this paper. The ablation study about these two blocks is exhibited in Sect. 4.2.

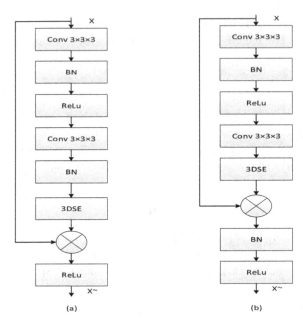

**Fig. 3.** (a) The architecture of BN-SE-Block; (b) The architecture of SE-BN-Block.

## 4   Experiments and Analysis

### 4.1   The Details of Datasets and Our Experiment

The proposed approach in this paper was evaluated on three challenging datasets, including HMDB51 [19], UCF101 [20], and Something-Something v1 [21] datasets. In our experiment, the SGD (Stochastic Gradient Descent) optimizer and the cross entropy loss function were used to optimize the parameters of networks. In this paper, a strategy of automatic adjustment of learning rate is adopted. Specially, the initial learning rate of the model is set to 0.001, and the learning rate is automatically decreased by factor 10 when the average top-1 accuracy on the validation set no longer achieves a larger value within 5 consecutive epochs. The model was pre-trained on the Kinetics [22] dataset and then fine-tuned on the HMDB51, UCF101, and Something-Something v1 datasets.

In order to choose a suitable value of N (the number of segments for a video, which can not only make full use of all the information of a video, but also reduce the input of redundant information), this section has experimented with the value of N. Specifically, in this chapter, ESENet is used as the benchmark model, and different values of N are verified on the HMDB51 dataset (N values are respectively 4, 8, 12, 16, 20, 24, 28, 32). The impact on the accuracy of the model is shown in Fig. 4. It can be seen from Fig. 4 that when N = 16, the model acquired the higher accuracy. Therefore, we set N = 16 in the all experiments.

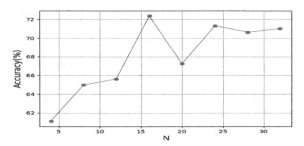

**Fig. 4.** Different settings of parameter N.

## 4.2 The Ablation Study

In order to find a more effective network structure, the ablation study is implemented. Two different 3D residual attention units, BN-SE-Block and SE-BN-Block, are respectively embedded into the ResNet34-3DRes18 network to form two different networks: ESENet(BN-SE) and ESENet(SE-BN). The two networks were respectively evaluated on the HMDB51 and UCF101 datasets, as shown in Table 1. In Table 1, its second and third column represents the top-1 accuracy of the two methods on the HMDB51 test set and the UCF101 split1 respectively. According to the Table 1, we can conclude that the ESENet(SE- BN) network achieved better performance than the ESENet(BN-SE) network on two datasets. Specially, the former achieved more 2.629% and 1.052% top-1 accuracy respectively on the two datasets than the later. This fully demonstrates that the SE-BN-Block residual attention unit is better than the BN-SE-Block in the video behavior recognition task.

**Table 1.** Comparing ESENet(SE-BN) with ESENet(BN-SE) on HMDB51 and UCF101 datasets.

| Methods | HMDB51(%) | UCF101(%) |
|---|---|---|
| ESENet(BN-SE) | 69.739 | 91.911 |
| ESENet(SE-BN) | 72.368(+2.629) | 92.963(+1.052) |

## 4.3 Comparing 3DSE with SE

In order to demonstrate the advantages of 3DSE than SE in the video behavior recognition task, Res34-SE-IM-Net and ESENet are compared respectively on the HMDB51, UCF101, and Something-Something v1 datasets, as shown in Table 2. It is easily to find that the ESENet network outperforms the Res34-SE-IM-Net on the three datasets. Specially, the former achieved more 0.518%, 0.767%, and 0.191% top-1 accuracy respectively than the latter. This effectively demonstrates that the 3DSE module has an advantage than the SE module in spatial feature channels recalibration of videos.

**Table 2.** Comparing Res34-SE-IM-Net with ESENet on HMDB51, UCF101, Something-Something v1 datasets.

| Methods | HMDB51(%) | UCF101(%) | Something- Something v1 (%) |
|---|---|---|---|
| Res34-SE-IM-Net (16frames) [16] | 71.85 | 92.196 | 41.398 |
| ESENet(16 frames) | 72.368(**+0.518**) | 92.963(**+0.767**) | 41.589(**+0.191**) |

### 4.4  The Comparison to Other Approaches on Different Datasets

The ESENet network was compared with other behavior recognition methods on the HMDB51, UCF101, and Something-Something v1 datasets, as shown in Table 3 and 4. In Table 3, the compared methods include the traditional methods based on artificial features and the approaches based on deep learning. The latter is divided into 2DCNN, 3DCNN, 2D + 3D CNN and other type of methods. The proposed method in this paper is at the end of the table. From Table 3, it is easily to see that the proposed method in this paper has achieved better performance than other kinds of methods except I3D and TSN. For I3D, it has a deeper network structure than ours. Specially, the I3D network has 72 layers including convolutional layer and pooling layer, but our network only has 50 layers (including SE layer). Meanwhile, our model has fewer the numbers of floating point operations (FLOPs) than I3D, 85.57G and 153G respectively. This made our model could converge faster and complete training. For TSN, the accuracy of our model is more 3.868% in the HMDB51 dataset, but is less 1.037% in the UCF101 dataset. In Table 4, the proposed method is compared with other methods on the Something-Something v1 dataset. And it acquired 41.589% top-1 accuracy which is better than other approaches.

**Table 3.**  Comparison to the state-of-the-art on HMDB51,UCF101 datasets.

| Type | Method | Input modality | Pre-training | HMDB51(%) | UCF101(%) |
|---|---|---|---|---|---|
| Traditional | IDT [4] | RGB | – | 57.2 | 85.9 |
| Traditional | MIFS [23] | RGB | – | 65.1 | 89.1 |
| 2DCNN | Two-stream [7] | RGB Optical flow | ILSVRC | 59.4 | 88.0 |
| 2DCNN | TSN [17] | RGB Optical flow | ImageNet | 68.5 | 94.0 |
| 3DCNN | C3D + SVM [9] | RGB | Sports-1M | – | 85.2 |
| 3DCNN | I3D [10] | RGB | Kinetics | 74.5 | 95.4 |

*(continued)*

**Table 3.** (*continued*)

| Type | Method | Input modality | Pre-training | HMDB51(%) | UCF101(%) |
|------|--------|----------------|--------------|-----------|-----------|
| 3DCNN | Res3D [12] | RGB | Sports-1M | 54.9 | 85.8 |
| 2D + 3DCNN | ECO-Lite (16 frames) [11] | RGB | Kinetics | 68.2 | 91.6 |
| 2D + 3DCNN | ECO (16 frames) [11] | RGB | Kinetics | 68.5 | 92.8 |
| Other | FAST-3D (ResNet-101) [24] | RGB | ImageNet | 48.01 | 84.79 |
| Other | VGG + TSN [25] | RGB Optical flow | ImageNet | 67.3 | 92.1 |
| Other | RSN [26] | RGB | Kinetics | 53.6 | 90.1 |
| Other | SE-LRCN [2] | RGB | ImageNet | 50.98 | 82.49 |
| Our methods | ESENet (16 frames) | RGB | Kinetics | 72.368 | 92.963 |

**Table 4.** Comparison to the sate-of-the-art on Something-Something v1 dataset.

| Methods | Input modality | Pre-training | Top-1 val (%) |
|---------|----------------|--------------|---------------|
| ECO (16 frames) [11] | RGB | Kinetics | 41.4 |
| MultiScale TRN [27] | RGB | ImageNet | 34.44 |
| ESENet (16 frames) | RGB | Kinetics | 41.589 |

## 5 Conclusion

In this paper, the 3DSE module is integrated into the ResNet34-3DRes18 network in order to construct an ESENet model for human behavior recognition in videos. Different with the SE module, 3DSE fully takes into account the temporal information of videos. And this is advantageous for behavior recognition in videos. Furthermore, as different integration strategies have different influence, so how the 3DSE is integrated into the 3DRes18 is also discussed. Compared with the other behavior recognition methods, the ESENet network has achieved better results on three challenging public datasets. All of these fully proved the effectiveness of the proposed method. Although the ESENet network has acquired some results on video behavior recognition task, the model only pay attention to the influence from different spatial feature channels but not take the importance of different frames in a video into account. Therefore, we will consider to design and add a temporal attention module which can effectively distinguish the importance of different frames in a video in our future work.

**Acknowledgements.** This work was supported in part by the National Natural Science Foundation of China (Nos. U1908214, 91748104), Program for the Liaoning Distinguished Professor, the Scientific Research fund of Liaoning Provincial Education Department (No.L2019606), and the Science and Technology Innovation Fund of Dalian(No. 2020JJ25CY001, 2020JJ26GX034).

# References

1. Hu, J., Shen, L., Sun, G: Squeeze-and-excitation networks. In: Proceedings of CVPR, 2018, pp. 7132–7141, Salt Lake. IEEE Computer Society (2018)
2. An, G., Zhou, W., Wu, Y., et al.: Squeeze-and-excitation on spatial and temporal deep feature space for action recognition. arXiv:1806.00631 [cs.CV] (2018)
3. Zhu, W.T., Huang, Y.F., Zeng, L., et al.: AnatomyNet: deep learning for fast and fully automated whole-volume segmentation of head and neck anatomy. arXiv:1808.05238 [cs.CV] (2018)
4. Wang, H., Schmid, C.: Action recognition with improved trajectories. In: Proceedings of ICCV, 2013, pp. 3551–3558, Sydney. IEEE Computer Society (2013)
5. Bobick, A.F., Davis, J.W.: The recognition of human movement using temporal templates. IEEE Trans. Pattern Anal. Mach. Intell. **23**(3), 257–267 (2001)
6. Zhu, J., Zhu, Z., Zou, W.: End-to-end video-level representation learning for action recognition. In: Proceedings of ICPR, 2018, pp. 645–650, Beijing. IEEE Computer Society (2018)
7. Simonyan, K., Zisserman, A.: Two-stream convolutional networks for action recognition in videos. In: Proceedings of the 27th International Conference on Neural Information Processing Systems, 2014, vol. 1, pp. 568–576. MIT Press, Cambridge (2014)
8. Feichtenhofer, C., Pinz, A., Zisserman, A.: Convolutional two-stream network fusion for video action recognition. In: Proceedings of CVPR, 2016, pp. 1933–1941, Las Vegas. IEEE Computer Society (2016)
9. Tran, D., Bourdev, L., Fergus, R., et al.: Learning spatiotemporal features with 3D convolutional networks. In: Proceedings of ICCV, 2015, pp. 4489–4497, Santiago. IEEE Computer Society (2015)
10. Carreira, J., Zisserman, A.: Quo Vadis. Action recognition? a new model and the kinetics dataset. In: Proceedings of CVPR, 2017, pp. 4724–4733, Hawaii. IEEE Computer Society (2017)
11. Zolfaghari, M., Singh, K., Brox, T.: ECO: efficient convolutional network for online video understanding. In: Ferrari, V., Hebert, M., Sminchisescu, C., Weiss, Y. (eds.) ECCV 2018. LNCS, vol. 11206, pp. 713–730. Springer, Cham (2018). https://doi.org/10.1007/978-3-030-01216-8_43
12. Tran, D., Ray, J., Shou, Z., et al.: ConvNet architecture search for spatiotemporal feature learning. arXiv:1708.05038 [cs.CV] (2017)
13. Xie, S., Sun, C., Huang, J., et al.: Rethinking spatiotemporal feature learning: speed-accuracy trade-offs in video classification. In: Ferrari, V., Hebert, M., Sminchisescu, C., Weiss, Y. (eds.) ECCV 2018. LNCS, vol. 11219, pp. 318–335. Springer, Cham (2018). https://doi.org/10.1007/978-3-030-01267-0_19
14. Jaderberg, M., Simonyan, K., Zisserman, A., et al.: Spatial transformer networks. In: Proceedings of the 28th International Conference on Neural Information Processing Systems, 2015, vol. 2, pp. 2017–2025. MIT Press, Cambridge (2015)
15. Donahue, J., Hendricks, L.A., Rohrbach, M., et al.: Long-term recurrent convolutional networks for visual recognition and description. IEEE Trans. Pattern Anal. Mach. Intell. **39**(4), 677–691 (2017)

16. Chen, L., Liu, R., Zhou, D.S., et al.: Fused behavior recognition model based on attention mechanism. Vis. Comput. Ind. Biomed. Art **3**(1), 1–10 (2020). https://doi.org/10.1186/s42 492-020-00045-x

17. Wang, L., Xiong, Y., Wang, Z., et al.: Temporal segment networks: towards good practices for deep action recognition. In: Leibe, B., Matas, J., Sebe, N., Welling, M. (eds.) ECCV 2016. LNCS, vol. 9912, pp. 20–36. Springer, Cham (2016). https://doi.org/10.1007/978-3-319-464 84-8_2

18. He, K., Zhang, X., Ren, S.: Deep residual learning for image recognition. In: Proceedings of CVPR, 2016, pp. 770–778, Las Vegas. IEEE Computer Society (2016)

19. Kuehne, H., Jhuang, H., Garrote, E., et al.: HMDB: a large video database for human motion recognition. In: Proceedings of ICCV, 2011, pp. 2556–2563, Barcelona Spain. IEEE Computer Society (2011)

20. Soomro, K., Zamir, A.R., Shah, M.: UCF101: A dataset of 101 human actions classes from videos in the wild. arXiv:1212.0402 [cs.CV] (2012)

21. Goyal, R., Kahou, S.E., Michalski, V., et al: The "something something" video database for learning and evaluating visual common sense. In: Proceedings of ICCV, 2017, pp. 5843–5851, Venice. IEEE Computer Society (2017)

22. Kay, W., Carreira, J., Simonyan, K., et al: The kinetics human action video dataset. arXiv: 1705.06950 [cs.CV] (2017)

23. Zhong, L.Z., Ming, L., Chong L.X., et al.: Beyond gaussian pyramid: multi-skip feature stacking for action recognition. In: Proceedings of CVPR, 2015, pp. 204–212, Boston. IEEE Computer Society (2015)

24. Stergiou, A., Poppe, R.: Spatio-temporal FAST 3D convolutions for human action recognition. arXiv:1909.13474v2 [cs.CV] (2019)

25. Yuan, Y., Wang, D., Wang, Q.: Memory–augmented temporal dynamic learning for action recognition. arXiv:1904.13080v1 [cs.CV] (2019)

26. Wu, C., Cao, H., Zhang, W., et al.: Refined spatial network for human action recognition. IEEE Access **7**, 111043–111052 (2019)

27. Zhou, B., Andonian, A., Oliva, A., Torralba, A.: Temporal relational reasoning in videos. In: Ferrari, V., Hebert, M., Sminchisescu, C., Weiss, Y. (eds.) ECCV 2018. LNCS, vol. 11205, pp. 831–846. Springer, Cham (2018). https://doi.org/10.1007/978-3-030-01246-5_49

# Interpolating Frames
# for Super-Resolution Smoke Simulation
# with GANs

Wenguo Wei and Shiguang Liu[✉]

College of Intelligence and Computing, Tianjin University, Tianjin, China
`lsg@tju.edu.cn`

**Abstract.** Deep neural networks have enabled super-resolution of fluid data, which can successfully expand data from 2D to 3D. However, it is non-trivial to solve the incoherence between the super-resolution frames. In this paper, we introduce a new frame-interpolation method based on a conditional generative adversarial network for smoke simulation. Our model generates several intermediate frames between the original two consecutive frames to remove the incoherence. Specifically, we design a new generator that consists of residual blocks and a U-Net architecture. The generator with residual blocks is able to accurately recover high-resolution volumetric data from down-sampled one. We then input the two recovered frames and their corresponding velocity fields to the U-Net, warping and linearly fusing to generate several intermediate frames. Additionally, we propose a slow-fusion model to design our temporal discriminator. This model allows our adversarial network to progressively merge a series of consecutive frames step by step. The experiments demonstrate that our model could produce high-quality intermediate frames for smoke simulation, which efficiently remove the incoherence from the original fluid data.

**Keywords:** Deep learning · Frame interpolation · Smoke simulation · Temporal coherence.

## 1 Introduction

Super-resolution is a kind of techniques that enhances the resolution of input data. In recent years, this technique has been solved well with GANs. Inspired by this, TempoGAN [16] was proposed to apply super-resolution on fluid simulations. In order to increase the temporal consistency, TempoGAN incorporates an additional temporal discriminator to train the network. However, this method is not capable of eradicating the root of temporal incoherence problem, especially when the resolution is very large.

In this paper, we extend the generative ability of GANs to implement the frame-interpolation function, which is able to increase the smoothness between frames and alleviate the flickering phenomenon caused by the incoherence.

© Springer Nature Switzerland AG 2020
F. Tian et al. (Eds.): CASA 2020, CCIS 1300, pp. 14–21, 2020.
https://doi.org/10.1007/978-3-030-63426-1_2

Our generator takes two consecutive frames as input, including density field and velocity field. We employed four residual blocks to implement the super-resolution and the classical U–Net architecture with skip connections to generate intermediate frames.

Since the training data are consecutive frames, we employ a temporal discriminator in addition to the spatial discriminator. In order to increase the ability of mining temporal information, we adopt the slow-fusion model to construct the discriminator. The number of convolutional layers is determined by the input frames. The temporal information is extracted from a couple of consecutive frames, and we merge adjacent two of them each time. In this way, deeper temporal information would be found out, and help the discriminator to more accurately tell the authenticity of the output.

To summarize, the main contributions of our work are:

- A new generative adversarial network that aims to solve the super-resolution and frame incoherence problems in 2D and 3D smoke simulations.
- A novel generator to synthesize multiple intermediate frames is proposed, which could efficiently tackle the incoherence problem between the super-resolution frames.
- The slow-fusion model is taken as the structure of the temporal discriminator. This could extract more temporal information from the input, which is beneficial to train the generator.

## 2   Related Work

The traditional super-resolution methods are mainly based on interpolation or sparse representation [17]. In recent years, the super-resolution technique has achieved huge breakthroughs with the help of faster and deeper convolutional neural networks. However, these methods mainly focus on natural images or videos [4,6,7]. TempoGAN is the first approach to solve the super-resolution of four-dimensional volumetric data. Although TempoGAN successfully works out the physics fields with neural networks, it fails to solve the incoherence between frames. Based on the above observation, we propose a new generator with intermediate frame interpolation function.

Interpolation has been exploited in several previous traditional fluid simulation methods. Thuerey [14] employed a five-dimensional optical flow solver to precompute volumetric deformations. Raveendran et al. [9] proposed a semi-automatic method for matching two existing liquid animations as user guidance. Sato et al. [11] applied interpolation to edit or combine the original fluids. The above interpolation algorithms are designed for spatial dimension, which are not suitable for solving the temporal incoherent problems. The idea of combining deep learning with interpolation is more common in the field of image processing. The Super-SloMo algorithm trains an end-to-end convolutional neural network to interpolate arbitrary number of intermediate frames in a video [3]. We get inspiration from this paper and expand two-dimension image data interpolation to three-dimension fluid data interpolation.

More recently, deep-learning-based methods have been introduced into computing graphics. For example, convolutional neural networks were used to replace the pressure solve step [15], a CNN-based feature descriptor was proposed to synthesize new smoke flows [1], a regression forest was applied to approximate the behaviour of particles [5], and Hu et al. [2] proposed an interactive system to generate 2D fluid animation from hand-drawn sketches with conditional GAN.

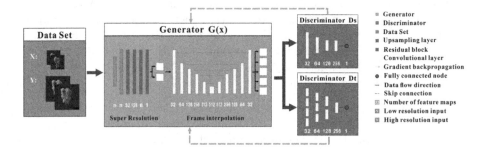

**Fig. 1.** A detailed overview of our network

## 3   Proposed Approach

### 3.1   Interpolating Frames

For the generator $G$, we take the two consecutive frames $\{X_0, X_1\}$ as input, and generate the high-resolution output $\{G(X_0), G(X_{t_1}), G(X_{t_2}), G(X_{t_3}), G(X_1)\}$, in which the three intermediate results are interpolated frames. We employ two upsampling layers and four residual blocks to implement super-resolution. The input data is upsampled with a factor of 4 through the first two layers. Then, we employ four residual blocks to refine the upsampled data. Each residual block consists of two convolutional layers with ReLU activation and a shortcut connection layer. In terms of interpolating intermediate frames, the consecutive two frames from the super-resolution module are input to the U-Net architecture. We denote them as $F_0$ and $F_1$, respectively. Then, we use the backward warping algorithm [8] to compute the intermediate frame between $F_0$ and $F_1$, which is denoted as $F_t$, $t \in (0,1)$. Then, $F_t$ could be synthesized by the following formulation:

$$F_t = (1 - t)W(F_0, V(t - 0)) + tW(F_1, V(t - 1)) \tag{1}$$

where $W$ is the backward warping function, which can be implemented with bilinear interpolation [8]. $V(t-0)$ is the velocity field from $F_t$ to $F_0$ and $V(t-1)$ is the velocity field from $F_t$ to $F_1$. The parameter $t$ is used as controlling factor: if $t$ is closer to 0 or 1, $F_0$ or $F_1$ will contribute more to $F_t$. Since the time step between two key frames is very small, we could approximate $V(t-0)$ and $V(t-1)$

with the help of velocity fields at $t = 0$ and $t = 1$, which is denoted as $V_0$ and $V_1$. We first estimate the velocity field $V_t$ at time $t$:

$$V_t = (1 - t)V_0 + tV_1 \qquad (2)$$

Then $V(t - 0)$ should be equal to $V_t$ but has the opposite direction: $V(t - 0) = -V_t$. And, $V(t - 1)$ can be assumed to $V_t : V(t - 1) = V_t$. With the density fields $F_0$, $F_1$ and velocity fields $V(t - 0)$, $V(t - 1)$, intermediate frames $F_t(t = 0.25, 0.5, 0.75)$ are computed. Then, these frames are fed to the U-Net [10] for training.

The U-Net architecture consists of two parts: encoder (left) and decoder (right), with skip connections between them. We employ 6 convolutional blocks in the encoder, each of which includes two convolutional layers, a Leaky ReLU layer and an average pooling layer. Five convolutional blocks are used in the decoder. Each block contains one upsampling layer, two convolutional layers and a Leaky ReLU layer.

### 3.2    Slow Fusion

Since fluid data is usually four dimensional including space (3D) and time (1D), our network employs two discriminators: spatial discriminator ($D_s$) and temporal discriminator ($D_t$). The spatial discriminator employs four simple convolutional layers. For the time dimension, the input data is multiple consecutive frames. This paper employs the slow fusion model to extract temporal information. Different from the direct convolution with four layers, our discriminator handles the input data with a hierarchical structure. While the data slowly passes through the network, temporal information is fused in pairs until all the frames are merged into one. The detailed network structure can be found in Fig. 1 (Discriminator ($D_t$)). In our case, the number of input frames is 5. For

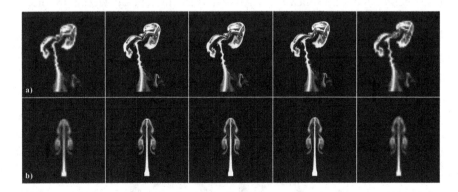

**Fig. 2.** The overview of two 2D smoke simulations generated with our model. The left and right columns are the low resolution input, and the three columns in the middle are the super-resolution intermediate frames(at time $t = 0.25, t = 0.5$ and $t = 0.75$, respectively)

the next steps, we merge two consecutive frames or feature maps in groups until the number goes down to 1. In our case, the number of features of each layer is 32, 64, 128, 256. The last layer is the fully connected node to make a judgment.

### 3.3   Loss Functions

In order to express the general idea of adversarial training, we employ a sigmoid cross entropy to train the discriminator $D_t$:

$$L_{D_t} = -E_m \left[\log D_t(Y_m)\right] - E_n \left[\log(1 - D_t(G(x_n)))\right] \tag{3}$$

and the discriminator $D_s$:

$$L_{D_s} = -E_m \left[\log D_s(Y_m)\right] - E_n \left[\log(1 - D_s(G(x_n)))\right] \tag{4}$$

For the training of generator $G$, we additionally adopt the construction loss $L_r$ and perceptual loss $L_p$. The complete loss function is defined as:

$$L_{r,p} = \alpha \left\|\hat{F}_t - Y_t\right\|_1 + \beta \left\|\Phi(\hat{F}_t) - \Phi(Y_t)\right\|_2 \tag{5}$$

where $F_t$ is the generated frames, and $Y_t$ is the corresponding ground truth. $\Phi$ denotes the *conv4_3* features of an ImageNet pretrained VGG16 model [12]. $\alpha$ and $\beta$ are the weighting factors. In our case, both of them are set to be 1. Then, the whole loss function of generator G is defined as:

$$L_G = \log(D_t(G(x_n))) + \log(D_s(G(x_n))) + L_{r,p} \tag{6}$$

## 4   Data Generation and Training

To train our network, we employed the popular fluid solver [13] to generate 2D and 3D training data. Specifically, we generated 15 different smoke simulations by

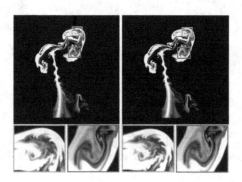

**Fig. 3.** The comparison between the generated intermediate frame (left) and the corresponding ground truth (right). The red and blue rectangles highlight the small scale details of smoke vortex and the bottom row is the close view of the local areas. (Color figure online)

the variant buoyancy and inflow velocity, each of which contains 200 frames. Each frame includes density field and velocity field. For convenience, we downscaled the high-resolution data to achieve the low-resolution version. The factor is set to be 0.25. We used two Nvidia GeForce GTX 1080Ti GPUs and Intel Core i9 CPU to train our model. For the 2D model, the training time is about 1 day. And the 3D model takes around 10 days.

## 5   Results

Figure 2 shows the intermediate frames generated by our model. These results demonstrate that our model could not only produce very detailed super-resolution smoke, but also generate intermediate frames with correct behavior and same resolution. Figure 3 shows the comparison between the generated intermediate frame and the corresponding ground truth. As can be seen in the figure, our model could produce the result that is highly similar to the ground truth. Figure 4 verifies the effectiveness of our slow fusion model. Our result is more smooth in terms of smoke density, especially in the rising plume area.

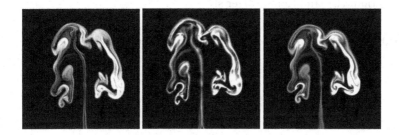

**Fig. 4.** The comparison of 2D smoke simulation with slow-fusion. On the left is the result without slow-fusion, in the middle is the result implemented with our algorithm and on the right is the ground truth

**Fig. 5.** An overview of 3D smoke simulation result. The left and right frames are low resolution input, and the three middle frames are the high resolution output corresponding to different times.

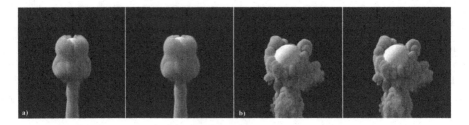

**Fig. 6.** The experiments of two smoke simulations with obstacles. For each group, the left is the generated result and the right is the corresponding ground truth.

Figure 5 exhibits the 3D smoke generated by our model. Figure 6 shows different 3D smoke simulations interacted with obstacles. It can be seen that the smoke maintains the correct shape and behaviour around the sphere. This demonstrates the compatibility of our model to deal with different types of smoke simulations interacting with obstacles. Table 1 collects the average time cost of different smoke simulations compared to TempoGAN. Our method has almost the same efficiency with TempoGAN, but the time cost of generating intermediate frames is far less than the traditional solver's.

**Table 1.** The average time cost of different smoke simulations per frame

|    |            | Resolution | TempoGAN  | Ours      |
|----|------------|------------|-----------|-----------|
| 2D | Fig. 2 (a) | $1024^2$   | 0.23 s    | 0.32 s    |
|    | Fig. 2 (b) | $1024^2$   | 0.24 s    | 0.31 s    |
|    | Fig. 5 (a) | $1024^2$   | 0.23 s    | 0.31 s    |
|    | Fig. 5 (b) | $256^2$    | 0.02 s    | 0.02 s    |
| 3D | Fig. 6     | $512^3$    | 5.03 min  | 5.27 min  |
|    | Fig. 7 (a) | $512^3$    | 5.05 min  | 5.28 min  |
|    | Fig. 7 (b) | $512^3$    | 5.06 min  | 5.28 min  |

## 6   Conclusions and Future Work

We have realized a conditional GAN to produce intermediate frames for smoke simulation, which could greatly alleviate the temporal incoherence between super-resolution results. We used four residual networks to implement the super-resolution. And for intermediate frame interpolation, we employed a U-Net architecture with skip connections. In order to increase the temporal coherence, we designed a temporal discriminator with the slow fusion model. Compared to the original simulations, our result has little flickering phenomenon and is visually smoother. In the future, our research aims to increase the number of intermediate frames, so that we could use fewer original frames generated by traditional solvers to achieve smoother smoke simulations. Also, simplifying the structure of our network to shorten the training time is under consideration.

**Acknowledgments.** The authors would like to thank the anonymous reviewers for their insightful comments. This work was supported by the National Key R&D Program of China under no. 2018YFC1407405, and the Natural Science Foundation of China under grant nos. 61672375 and 61170118.

# References

1. Chu, M., Thuerey, N.: Data-driven synthesis of smoke flows with cnn-based feature descriptors. ACM Trans. Graph. **36**(4), 1–4 (2017)
2. Hu, Z., Xie, H., Fukusato, T., Sato, T., Igarashi, T.: Sketch2vf: sketch-based flow design with conditional generative adversarial network. Comput. Animation and Virtual Worlds **30**(3–4), e1889 (2019)
3. Jiang, H., Sun, D., Jampani, V., Yang, M., Learned-Miller, E.G., Kautz, J.: Super slomo: high quality estimation of multiple intermediate frames for video interpolation. CoRR arXiv:abs/1712.00080 (2017)
4. Jo, Y., Oh, S., Kang, J., Kim, S.: Deep video super-resolution network using dynamic upsampling filters without explicit motion compensation. In: IEEE Conference on Computer Vision and Pattern Recognition (CVPR), pp. 3224–3232 (2018)
5. Ladický, L., Jeong, S., Solenthaler, B., Pollefeys, M., Gross, M.: Data-driven fluid simulations using regression forests. ACM Trans. Graph. **34**(6), 1–9 (2015)
6. Ledig, C., et al.: Photo-realistic single image super-resolution using a generative adversarial network. CoRR abs/1609.04802 (2016)
7. Lim, B., Son, S., Kim, H., Nah, S., Lee, K.: Enhanced Deep Residual Networks for Single Image Super-Resolution, pp. 1132–1140 (2017)
8. Liu, Z., Yeh, R.A., Tang, X., Liu, Y., Agarwala, A.: Video frame synthesis using deep voxel flow. In: IEEE International Conference on Computer Vision (ICCV), pp. 4473–4481 (2017)
9. Raveendran, K., Wojtan, C., Thuerey, N., Turk, G.: Blending liquids. ACM Trans. Graph. **33**(4), 1–10 (2014)
10. Ronneberger, O., Fischer, P., Brox, T.: U-net: convolutional networks for biomedical image segmentation. ArXiv arXiv:abs/1505.04597 (2015)
11. Sato, S., Dobashi, Y., Nishita, T.: Editing fluid animation using flow interpolation. ACM Trans. Graph. **37**(5), 173 (2018)
12. Simonyan, K., Zisserman, A.: Very deep convolutional networks for large-scale image recognition. arXiv 1409.1556 (2014)
13. Stam, J.: Stable fluids. In: Proceedings of SIGGRAPH, pp. 121–128 (1999)
14. Thuerey, N.: Interpolations of smoke and liquid simulations. ACM Trans. Graph. (TOG) **36**(1), 16 (2016)
15. Tompson, J., Schlachter, K., Sprechmann, P., Perlin, K.: Accelerating Eulerian Fluid Simulation With Convolutional Networks. ArXiv e-prints (2016)
16. Xie, Y., Franz, E., Chu, M., Thuerey, N.: Tempogan: a temporally coherent, volumetric gan for super-resolution fluid flow. ACM Trans. Graph. **37**(4), 95 (2018)
17. Yang, J., Wright, J., Huang, T.S., Yi, M.: Image super-resolution as sparse representation of raw image patches. In: IEEE Conference on Computer Vision and Pattern Recognition (CVPR), Anchorage, Alaska, USA (2008)

# 3D Face Reconstruction and Semantic Annotation from Single Depth Image

Peixin Li[1], Yuru Pei[1(✉)], Yuke Guo[2], and Hongbin Zha[1]

[1] Key Laboratory of Machine Perception (MOE), Department of Machine Intelligence, Peking University, Beijing, China
`peiyuru@cis.pku.edu.cn`
[2] Luoyang Institute of Science and Technology, Luoyang, China

**Abstract.** We introduce a novel data-driven approach for taking a single-view noisy depth image as input and inferring a detailed 3D face with per-pixel semantic labels. The critical point of our method is its ability to handle the depth completions with varying extent of geometric details, managing 3D expressive face estimation by exploiting low-dimensional linear subspace and dense displacement field-based non-rigid deformations. We devise a deep neural network-based coarse-to-fine 3D face reconstruction and semantic annotation framework to produce high-quality facial geometry while preserving large-scale contexts and semantics. We evaluate the semantic consistency constraint and the generative model for 3D face reconstruction and depth annotation in extensive series of experiments. The results demonstrate that the proposed approach outperforms the compared methods not only in the face reconstruction with high-quality geometric details, but also semantic annotation performances regarding segmentation and landmark location.

**Keywords:** Face reconstruction · Semantic annotation · Single-view depth image

## 1 Introduction

Single image-based 3D face estimation is a fundamental issue in the computer vision and graphics community with a variety of practical applications in animation and virtual reality [1], face recognition [6], and auto-driving [4]. This paper focuses on the challenging problem of high-quality 3D face reconstruction from a single noisy depth image, independent of color or intensity images with facial textures.

The depth image obtained from the consumer depth camera provides partial geometry and is invariant to illumination variations. However, the depth images are limited in quality, with depth missing due to occlusions and device-specific noise. The unpleasant holes exist on facial surfaces in the single-view depth image. Furthermore, it is hard to handle the non-rigid expressive deformations, such as the big mouth, due to the lack of semantic textural constraints in depth

© Springer Nature Switzerland AG 2020
F. Tian et al. (Eds.): CASA 2020, CCIS 1300, pp. 22–30, 2020.
https://doi.org/10.1007/978-3-030-63426-1_3

images. Traditional methods employ the Poisson surface reconstruction [10] and the Laplacian mesh editing [11] for the hole filling and denoising. Although there is significant progress in depth-based facial structure tracking [4,7], the reconstructed 3D face quality is not satisfactory regarding deformable facial structures.

One promising direction towards the single-view-based 3D face reconstruction is to use a data-driven machine learning method to handle the ill-posed problem. The learning-based parametric model bridges the depth image with facial pose parameters [7]. Very recently, the deep learning-based methods for 3D face reconstruction has shown promising results [15,16]. Compared with traditional hand-crafted features, the deep neural network (DNN) shows excellent capacity in feature learning and building the mapping between 2D images and 3D faces. A DNN-based Poseidon [4] realized depth image-based 3D face estimation by a face-from-depth model. The 3D morphable model (3DMM) [3] is the mainstream deformable facial representation for its low-dimensional parametric space and model compactness. However, the 3DMM often produces a smooth face with limited principal components to capture geometric details. The coarse-to-fine model handles the recovery of fine-grained facial details, which relies on the shape-from-shading techniques to recover geometric details from color images [15,18]. Whereas, the depth image does not bear the textures for semantic structure reconstruction.

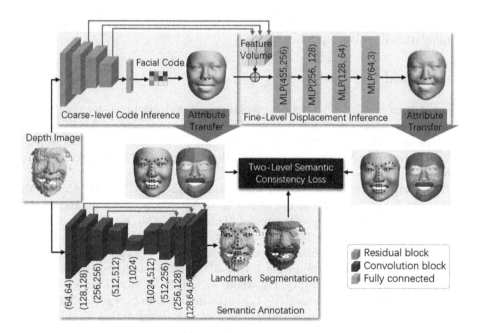

**Fig. 1.** Overview of the proposed coarse-to-fine 3D face estimation and per-pixel semantic annotation from a single-view depth image. We introduce a two-level structure consistency constraint to enforce the semantic correspondence between the 3D face and the input depth image.

In this paper, we propose a novel data-driven approach for taking a single-view noisy depth image as the input and predicting a 3D face with per-pixel semantic labels, without resorting to textures in color or intensity images. We utilize a cascaded DNN-based coarse-to-fine framework for the 3D face geometry, leveraging both low-dimensional linear subspace and the dense displacement field. A residual network is used to infer coarse 3DMM-based facial geometry, which is learned from both synthetic and real depth images. We further infer per-vertex displacements for recovering the facial details in an unsupervised manner. We introduce a two-level structure consistency constraint to enforce semantic correspondence between the 3D face and the input depth image. The semantic annotations, including landmarks and feature segmentation, inferred by the annotation network, are required to be consistent with label propagation from the coarse- and fine-level reconstructed 3D faces.

In our evaluations, we show 3D face reconstruction and per-pixel semantic annotation of depth images. We demonstrate that it is possible to apply the model to noisy depth images obtained by the consumer depth camera for high-quality face reconstruction. The results outperform the compared state-of-the-art methods. In summary, the contributions are as follows:

– We devise a DNN-based coarse-to-fine framework to produce high-quality 3D face with geometric details and large-scale geometric contexts from a single depth image.
– We introduce a two-level structure consistency scheme for semantic corre-spondence between the 3D face and the depth image, realizing the per-pixel annotation of noisy depth images.

## 2    Method

Our goal is to predict a 3D detailed facial model and per-pixel semantic anno-tations from a single-view depth image. We introduce a coarse-to-fine 3D recon-struction network to predict low-dimensional shape parameters and dense per-vertex displacements for non-rigid registration of a parametric 3D face and the noisy depth image.

As shown in Fig. 1, our system takes one depth image $I \in \mathbb{R}^{N_p}$ with $N_p$ pixels as an input and outputs the global 3DMM-based facial parameters in the coarse level, which uniquely determine a 3D face mesh $M_c(V_c, E)$ with vertices $V_c \in \mathbb{R}^{3N_v}$ and edges $E \in \mathbb{R}^{3N_e}$. $N_v$ and $N_e$ indicate the number of vertexes and triangle edges. In the fine level, the network takes the vertex set $V_c$ of the coarse facial mesh and outputs per-vertex 3D displacements field $U \in \mathbb{R}^{3N_v}$. The resulting facial mesh $M_f(V_f, E)$, where $V_f = V_c + U$. Moreover, our system produces per-pixel annotations $Y(Y_l, Y_r)$ of the input depth images, including the landmarks $Y_l \in \mathbb{R}^{N_p \times n_l}$ of $n_l$ landmarks and feature segmentation $Y_r \in \mathbb{R}^{N_p \times n_r}$ of $n_r$ regions of interest. $Y$ is binary labeling assigned to each pixel with 1 of the landmark or the foreground region and 0 otherwise.

The proposed framework consists of three subnetworks: the coarse-level facial code inference subnetwork, the fine-level displacement prediction subnetwork, and the semantic annotation subnetwork. We learn the proposed network using both the noisy depth image dataset $\mathcal{I}_u$ captured by the consumer depth camera Kinect and the synthetic depth image dataset $\mathcal{I}_a$ with ground-truth face codes and annotations.

## 2.1 Coarse-Level Facial Code Inference

We use the residual network [9] to parameterize the mapping function $f$ from the depth image to the global low-dimensional facial codes of the 3DMM-based parametric face [3]. Given the input depth image $I$, the facial codes $(\alpha_p, \alpha_s, \alpha_e) = f(I)$. The 3D face

$$V_c = r(\bar{V} + \alpha_s \Phi_s + \alpha_e \Phi_e) + t. \tag{1}$$

$r \in SO(3)$ and $t \in \mathbb{R}^3$ denote the 3D rotation and translation. The pose code $\alpha_p = (r, t)$. $\bar{V}$ denotes the neutral 3D face. $\Phi_s \in \mathbb{R}^{3 \times N_v \times n_s}$ refers to the facial identity basis, the first $n_s$ dominant principal components learned from the Basel Face database [12]. $\Phi_e \in \mathbb{R}^{3 \times N_v \times n_e}$ denotes the expressive basis learned from the FaceWarehouse database [5]. We use the non-rigid ICP algorithm [2] to align the facial meshes of the Basel and the FaceWarehouse with different topologies. $\alpha_s \in \mathbb{R}^{n_s}$ and $\alpha_e \in \mathbb{R}^{n_e}$ denote the identity and expression parameters, where $n_s$ and $n_e$ are set to 80 and 64 respectively in experiments.

Both the synthetic depth image dataset $\mathcal{I}_a$ with ground-truth facial codes $(\alpha_p^*, \alpha_s^*, \alpha_e^*)$ and the un-annotated real depth image dataset $\mathcal{I}_u$ are used to learn the code inference network. We generate the synthetic dataset with $40k$ depth images by depth rendering of the morphable 3D face with randomly sampled pose, expression, and identity parameters. The loss function of the coarse-level code inference

$$\mathcal{L}_{cl} = \lambda_1 \sum_{I \in \mathcal{I}_a} \{\|\frac{\alpha_p - \alpha_p^*}{\sigma_p}\|_2^2 + \|\frac{\alpha_s - \alpha_s^*}{\sigma_s}\|_2^2 + \|\frac{\alpha_e - \alpha_e^*}{\sigma_e}\|_2^2\} + \sum_{I \in \mathcal{I}_u} \sum_{p \in \theta(I)} \min_{v \in V_c} \|v - p\|_2^2, \tag{2}$$

where the first part is the supervised learning loss concerning the synthetic dataset with ground-truth face codes. The predicted face code $(\alpha_p, \alpha_s, \alpha_e) = f(I)$. $\sigma_p$, $\sigma_s$, and $\sigma_e$ denote code variances of the pose, the identity, and the expression respectively. $\lambda_1$ is a hyper-parameter. The second part is the unsupervised fitting loss using real noisy depth images. $\theta(I)$ denotes the point cloud of the input depth image. The network parameters are optimized by minimizing the distance between the point clouds of the reconstructed 3D face $V_c$ and the input noisy depth image.

The code inference network produces the global low-dimensional facial codes, uniquely determining the 3D face. Whereas, the resulted face mesh is smooth and lacks local geometric details, such as wrinkles and folds, due to the limited principal components spanning the linear subspaces of identities and expressions.

## 2.2   Fine-Level Displacement Inference

In order to account for local geometric details, we further predict the dense per-vertex displacement field. The dense displacement prediction network takes the parametric face $V_c$ as the input and produces the displacement field $U \in \mathbb{R}^{3N_v}$ composed of the per-vertex 3D displacement vectors. The final output 3D face is computed as $V_f = V_c + U$.

We build the displacement prediction network similar to the PointNet [13] to embed the surface point cloud into global shape features and to predict the per-vertex displacement vectors. The input point clouds are enhanced by using multi-scale feature volumes of depth images, where the 3D point coordinates of the parametric face $V_c$ are concatenated with feature vectors of its corresponding pixels on the depth image. The loss function of the fine-level displacement inference is defined as follows:

$$\mathcal{L}_{fl} = \sum_{I \in \mathcal{I}_u} \sum_{p \in \theta(I)} \min_{v \in V_f} \|v - p\|_2^2 + \lambda_2 \sum_{u_i \in U} \sum_{(v_i, v_j) \in E} \|u_i - u_j\|_2^2. \tag{3}$$

The first term measures the distance between the deformed 3D face and the input depth image. The second smoothness term is used to minimize the displacement variations of neighboring vertexes. The hyper-parameter $\lambda_2$ balances the mesh smoothness and the data term related to the point cloud alignment.

## 2.3   Semantic Annotation

We build the U-net [14]-based semantic annotation network for landmark detection and feature segmentation, as shown in Fig. 1. The landmark detection and segmentation share the encoder-decoder network. We initialize the semantic annotation network by learning the network parameters from the synthetic depth image dataset $\mathcal{I}_a$ paired with per-pixel labels. The semantic annotation loss

$$\mathcal{L}_{sem} = \lambda_3 \sum_{i=1}^{n_l} \|y_{l,i} - y_{l,i}^*\|_2^2 - \sum_{j=1}^{n_r} y_{r,j} \log y_{r,j}^* + \lambda_4 \delta_{SC}, \tag{4}$$

where $y_{l,i}$ and $y_{r,j}$ denote the predicted heat map of landmark $i$ and the labeling probability of facial region $j$ respectively. $y^*$ refers to the ground truth.

The annotation model learned from the synthetic depth images is not enough to label the noisy ones captured by the consumer depth camera due to the domain shift. In this work, we train the annotation network by exploiting a two-level semantic consistency between the predicted per-pixel annotations and the parametric 3D face. $\delta_{SC}$ measures the $l_2$-norm-based labeling difference of landmarks and the cross-entropy-based segmentation variations, and $\delta_{SC} = \sum_{\kappa \in \{cl, fl\}} \{\lambda_5 \sum_{i=1}^{n_l} \|y_{l,i} - y_{l,i}^{\kappa'}\|_2^2 + \sum_{j=1}^{n_r} [-y_{r,j} \log y_{r,j}^{\kappa'} + \lambda_6 d_r(\mathcal{R}_j^{\theta(I)}, \mathcal{R}_i^{V_\kappa})]\}$. $y_l'$ and $y_r'$ denote attribute transfer-based labeling maps of the landmarks and feature segmentation. $d_r$ evaluates the point cloud distance between the feature region $\mathcal{R}_j^{\theta(I)}$ on the depth image and $\mathcal{R}_i^{V_\kappa}$ on the reconstructed 3D face.

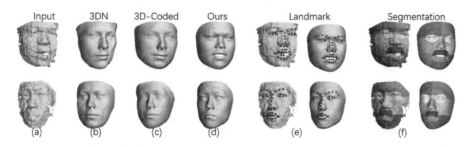

**Fig. 2.** 3D face reconstruction and semantic annotation from a single depth image. a) Input. (b) 3DN. (c) 3D-Coded. (d) Ours. (e) landmark location and (f) feature segmentation on both the depth image and the reconstructed 3D face.

### 2.4   Loss

The overall loss function of the proposed 3D face reconstruction and semantic annotation network is defined as follows:

$$\mathcal{L} = \gamma_{cl}\mathcal{L}_{cl} + \gamma_{fl}\mathcal{L}_{fl} + \gamma_{sem}\mathcal{L}_{sem}. \tag{5}$$

The hyper-parameters $\gamma_{cl}$, $\gamma_{fl}$, and $\gamma_{sem}$ are used to balance the coarse- and fine-level 3D face reconstruction, the per-pixel annotation, and semantic consistency constraints. The hyper-parameters $\lambda_1$, $\lambda_2$, $\lambda_3$, $\lambda_4$, $\lambda_5$, and $\lambda_6$ are set to 0.5, 5, 0.1, 4, 0.1, and 0.2 respectively. $\gamma_{cl}$, $\gamma_{fl}$, and $\gamma_{sem}$ are set to 1, 1, and 0.5.

## 3   Experiments

To evaluate the proposed approach, we send the depth images to the cascaded 3D reconstruction and semantic annotation network. Representative results on 3D face reconstruction with various head poses are shown in Fig. 2. We conduct the ablation studies on two-level semantic consistency constraints and compare it with state-of-the-art registration-based methods quantitatively and qualitatively. **Dataset and Metrics.** We use the consumer depth camera Kinect to obtain $20k$ depth images from 10 subjects with a resolution of $640 \times 480$, which is randomly split with $18k$ images for training and the remaining for testing. Both the training and the testing data are cropped to a resolution of $150 \times 150$ with face centered. We evaluate the 3D face reconstruction, landmark detection, and feature segmentation using three metrics. The face reconstruction accuracy $(RA)$ is computed using point distance between the 3D face $V$ and the point cloud $\theta(I)$ of the input depth image, and $RA = \frac{1}{|\theta(I)|}\sum_{p\in\theta(I)}\min_{v\in V}\|v - p\|_2$. The landmark detection accuracy $(LA)$ and segmentation accuracy $(SA)$ are computed as: $LA = \|v_l - v_l^*\|_2$, and $SA = \frac{2|\mathcal{R}\cap\mathcal{R}^*|}{|\mathcal{R}|+|\mathcal{R}^*|}$. $v_l$ and $v_l^*$ denote the detected and ground-truth landmarks. $SA$ is computed using the Dice similarity coefficients when given the estimated region of interest $\mathcal{R}$ and ground-truth $\mathcal{R}^*$.

As shown in Fig. 2, we compare our method with state-of-the-art learning-based registration methods, including the 3DN [17] and the 3D-Coded [8]. The

**Table 1.** Reconstruction accuracies ($RA$ (mm)) of compared methods.

|              | Avg. | Brow | Eye  | Nose | Mouth |
|--------------|------|------|------|------|-------|
| 3DN [17]     | 3.88 | 3.13 | 3.29 | 3.76 | 4.39  |
| 3D-Coded [8] | 2.09 | 1.87 | 2.01 | 2.80 | 3.55  |
| w/o SC       | 1.86 | 1.58 | 1.81 | 2.53 | 2.62  |
| with SC      | **1.82** | **1.53** | **1.76** | **2.47** | **2.54** |

fine-level reconstruction network is similar to the compared unsupervised registration networks [8,17]. However, we integrate the depth image features and the 3DMM-based coarse reconstruction to augment the input point cloud for the displacement inference. Moreover, we address the structure correspondence explicitly utilizing the semantic annotation subnetwork. Table 1 shows the quantitative comparisons on 3D face reconstruction. Thanks to the cascaded refinement scheme and the semantic correspondence, our method outperforms the compared methods regarding the $RA$ in all reported facial regions.

To validate the effects of two-level semantic consistency constraints, we build the 3D reconstruction and annotation networks with and without the semantic consistency constraints concerning both 3DMM-based coarse-level reconstructed face and the displacement-based fine-level one. We evaluate the facial reconstruction and the semantic annotation networks learned without semantic consistency constraints (w/o SC) and the one with the two-level consistency constraints (SC), as shown in Table 1 and Table 2. The face reconstruction and the semantic annotation network benefits from the structure consistency correspondence for the generalization to the real noisy images, unaffected by facial poses and expressions.

**Table 2.** Semantic annotation accuracies using variants of the proposed methods. Left: the $SA$ of the eye, the nose, the upper (U) lip, the lower (L) lip, the cheek, and the jaw. Right: the $LA$ (mm) of landmarks along the brow, the eye, the nose, and the upper (U) and lower (L) lips.

|         | SA   |      |      |       |       |       |      | LA (mm) |      |      |      |       |       |
|---------|------|------|------|-------|-------|-------|------|---------|------|------|------|-------|-------|
|         | Avg. | Eye  | Nose | U-Lip | L-Lip | Cheek | Jaw  | Avg.    | Brow | Eye  | Nose | U-Lip | L-Lip |
| w/o SC  | 0.75 | 0.77 | 0.80 | 0.64  | 0.59  | 0.74  | 0.77 | 8.41    | 8.75 | 8.35 | 6.55 | 9.00  | 9.43  |
| with SC | 0.87 | 0.86 | 0.88 | 0.87  | 0.81  | 0.86  | 0.87 | 4.67    | 5.01 | 3.45 | 4.47 | 4.86  | 6.16  |

## 4   Conclusion

We have proposed a DNN-based framework for 3D face estimation and semantic annotation from a single depth image. We propose a coarse-to-fine reconstruction framework with a cascaded low-dimensional code inference subnetwork and a high-dimensional displacement inference subnetwork to handle both global and local structure reconstruction. We present a two-level semantic consistency constraint, which enforces the semantic correspondence of the 3D face and the depth image and enables adaptation of the annotation network to noisy depth images. Quantitative and qualitative experiments show rationality of the cascaded framework and the two-level semantic consistency constraint on 3D face reconstruction and depth image annotation.

# References

1. Alexander, O., et al.: The digital emily project: achieving a photorealistic digital actor. IEEE CGA **30**(4), 20–31 (2010)
2. Amberg, B., Romdhani, S., Vetter, T.: Optimal step nonrigid ICP algorithms for surface registration. In: IEEE CVPR, pp. 1–8 (2007)
3. Blanz, V., Vetter, T.: A morphable model for the synthesis of 3D faces. In: SIG-GRAPH, pp. 187–194 (1999)
4. Borghi, G., Venturelli, M., Vezzani, R., Cucchiara, R.: Poseidon: face-from-depth for driver pose estimation. In: IEEE CVPR, pp. 5494–5503 (2017)
5. Cao, C., Weng, Y., Zhou, S., Tong, Y., Zhou, K.: Facewarehouse: a 3D facial expression database for visual computing. IEEE Trans. VCG **20**(3), 413–425 (2014)
6. Chu, B., Romdhani, S., Chen, L.: 3D-aided face recognition robust to expression and pose variations. In: IEEE CVPR, pp. 1899–1906 (2014)
7. Fanelli, G., Gall, J., Van Gool, L.: Real time head pose estimation with random regression forests. In: IEEE CVPR, pp. 617–624 (2011)
8. Groueix, T., Fisher, M., Kim, V.G., Russell, B.C., Aubry, M.: 3D-coded: 3D correspondences by deep deformation. In: ECCV (2018)
9. He, K., Zhang, X., Ren, S., Sun, J.: Deep residual learning for image recognition. In: IEEE CVPR, pp. 770–778 (2016)
10. Kazhdan, M., Bolitho, M., Hoppe, H.: Poisson surface reconstruction. In: Eurographics Symposium on Geometry processing, vol. 7 (2006)
11. Nealen, A., Igarashi, T., Sorkine, O., Alexa, M.: Laplacian mesh optimization. In: Proceedings of the 4th International Conference on Computer Graphics and Interactive Techniques in Australasia and Southeast Asia, pp. 381–389 (2006)
12. Paysan, P., Knothe, R., Amberg, B., Romdhani, S., Vetter, T.: A 3D face model for pose and illumination invariant face recognition. In: IEEE International Conference on Advanced Video and Signal Based Surveillance, pp. 296–301 (2009)
13. Qi, C.R., Su, H., Mo, K., Guibas, L.J.: Pointnet: deep learning on point sets for 3D classification and segmentation. arXiv preprint arXiv:1612.00593 (2016)
14. Ronneberger, O., Fischer, P., Brox, T.: U-Net: convolutional networks for biomedical image segmentation. In: Navab, N., Hornegger, J., Wells, W.M., Frangi, A.F. (eds.) MICCAI 2015. LNCS, vol. 9351, pp. 234–241. Springer, Cham (2015). https://doi.org/10.1007/978-3-319-24574-4_28
15. Tewari, A., et al.: Self-supervised multi-level face model learning for monocular reconstruction at over 250 hz. In: IEEE CVPR, pp. 2549–2559 (2018)

16. Tewari, A., et al.: Mofa: model-based deep convolutional face autoencoder for unsupervised monocular reconstruction. In: IEEE ICCV, vol. 2, p. 5 (2017)
17. Wang, W., Ceylan, D., Mech, R., Neumann, U.: 3dn: 3D deformation network. In: IEEE CVPR, pp. 1038–1046 (2019)
18. Yan, S., et al.: DDRNet: depth map denoising and refinement for consumer depth cameras using cascaded cnns. In: Ferrari, V., Hebert, M., Sminchisescu, C., Weiss, Y. (eds.) ECCV 2018. LNCS, vol. 11214, pp. 155–171. Springer, Cham (2018). https://doi.org/10.1007/978-3-030-01249-6_10

# A Robot for Interactive Glove Puppetry Performance

Yingying She[1], Xiaomeng Xu[1], Huahui Liu[1], Jiayu Lin[1], Minke Yang[2],
Lin Lin[2(✉)], and Baorong Yang[3(✉)]

[1] School of Informatics, Xiamen University, Xiamen, China
yingyingshe@xmu.edu.cn,
{24320181153624,24320181153622}@stu.xmu.edu.cn, 845681553@qq.com
[2] Art College, Xiamen University, Xiamen, China
2862675962@qq.com, linlinxiamen@xmu.edu.cn
[3] Computer Engineering College, Jimei University, Xiamen, China
yangbr2011@gmail.com

**Abstract.** A glove puppet is a puppet operated by an actor's hand. In China glove puppetry is a type of traditional opera with a thousand-year history. In this paper, a robot named HinHRob is presented to control a glove puppet in interactive puppetry performance. It introduces the structure and the control of motion of the robot in this paper, and presents an example to explain how HinHRob participates in the interactive performance. Questionnaires and interviews are employed to evaluate HinHRob's performance. The results show that HinHRob can effectively arouse audience's interest of performances and give audience immersive experience during the glove puppetry performance through different kinds of interaction.

**Keywords:** Robot · Interactive performance · Glove puppertry

## 1 Introduction

Jinjiang glove puppetry is a type of opera using glove puppets. It has integrated various techniques, arts and culture during its one thousand year of development history. It is a fruit of Chinese traditions. It is a popular entertainment activity for people in its prosperous years and often performed in folk festivals. In 2012, Jinjiang glove puppetry was listed as an "Intangible Cultural Heritage of Humanity".

However, like many other traditional arts, glove puppetry also falls into a bottleneck period. Along with many new kinds of entertainment which are more attractive, many problems of glove puppetry itself have been highlighted, such as the shrinking size of the troupe, the reduction of performances and the loss and aging of the audiences. As a result, the inheritance of glove puppetry is in danger.

In order to inherit traditional culture heritage like glove puppetry, it is important to popularize it among teenagers. In this paper, we present a robot namely

© Springer Nature Switzerland AG 2020
F. Tian et al. (Eds.): CASA 2020, CCIS 1300, pp. 31–40, 2020.
https://doi.org/10.1007/978-3-030-63426-1_4

HinHBob, which can play a glove puppet in performance. The participation of the robot can better arouse interest of the youth and improve traditional performances and so can help to promote the spread of this traditional art.

## 2    Related Work

With the rapid development of technology, audience interaction is more possible to be used in traditional performance. Enhancing the interactivity of performances can make the audience better integrate into performances and get a better sense of immersion compared with traditional performances [1,2]. Researchers have discussed audience's active participation in virtual performances [3,4]. New technology has also been used in glove puppetry performance. Way et al. [5] presented a glove puppetry cloud theater through a virtual reality work. Lin et al. [6] used Unity to create a virtual glove puppet which can be controlled with Leap Motion. Nitsche and McBride presented a bottom-up design exploration of traditional puppetry controls in VR. Traditional concept of audience and performers has gradually changed, and these interaction enhancements bring new challenges to HCI.

Robots can be an attractive and interesting interactive element in performances. With development of arm simulation [7] and bipedal robots [8,9], some researchers tried to use robots in performance. Polyak [10] presented a digital double of a physical puppet that is controlled by a performance interface designed specifically for glove puppets. Similarly, Lin et al. [6] proposed a human-marionette interaction system for interactive artistic puppetry and a mimicking-marionette game.

Although there have been some examples of robots used in performance, it is still a far way for exploring how to use robots to expand performance pattern. In this paper, a robot namely HinHRob is proposed to bring some novelty to traditional glove puppetry in an interactive way. For one hand, it is used for enhancing the interaction with users by a designed interactive performance. For the other hand, it can enhance the interaction between the actors and the audience.

## 3    Method

The process of the control system in the interactive glove puppetry performance is shown in Fig. 1. After being collected by acquisition equipment, body gestures, spatial movement(position and orientation) and hand gestures of users are sent to strategy module. Then a state machine is used in the strategy algorithm to generate the motion vectors which will later be used for computing the motions of the robot. Different states are set based on the actors' motion guidance. Different vectors represent different posture of the robot. Based on the current posture of the robot and the target motion vector, a motion computation module adjusts the concrete motions for the robot so that the robot can make smooth motions. At last, the robot receives computation result from the strategy module and

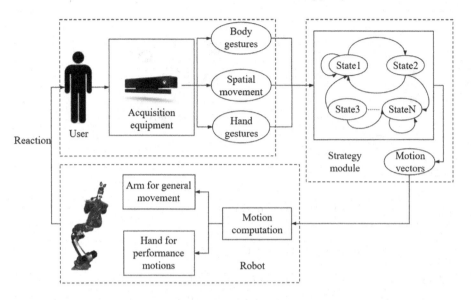

**Fig. 1.** The process of the control system.

moves with what the computation module tells. The robot consists of arm and hand, while the arm of the robot controls general movement of the robot and the hand part controls concrete performance motions.

### 3.1    Robot

The operation of glove puppets needs professional skills. To the best of our knowledge, there is no existing robot for glove puppetry. Therefore a robot for puppet control named HinHRob is developed [11]. As shown in Fig. 2, the robot is composed of two parts: arm and hand, and these two parts respectively simulate humans' arm and hand.

The arm part controls the general movement of the puppet and simulates real actors' body gesture. It has three components corresponding to humans body, elbow and wrist. The arm part has six rotatable joints and each joint has its own range of rotation (as Table 1 shows). The general gesture of puppets is controlled by changes of these six joints angle. The hand part controls motions of the puppet itself. It has seven joints corresponding to the puppets head, shoulders and limbs. Table 2 shows the range of rotation and corresponding part of the hand part. Different performance motions of the puppet are done by adjusting these joints of the hand part.

Robots and actors both have their own advantages. In practice HinHRob can do some exaggerated motions that actors cannot do and professional actors can do some soft and graceful motions. So it is necessary to consider different features of the robot and actors in the interactive glove puppetry performance.

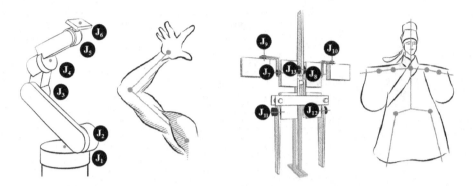

**Fig. 2.** Structure of HinHRob. It is composed of arm and hand which has 6 and 7 joints respectively.

**Table 1.** Range of rotation of each joint in arm.

| Joint ID | J1 | J2 | J3 | J4 | J5 | J6 |
|---|---|---|---|---|---|---|
| Origin angle | −122 | 29 | −70 | 19.8 | −52 | −18 |
| Range of rotation | −142–38 | 9–87 | −133--52 | 8.3–63.3 | −81--16 | −133–172 |

**Table 2.** Range of rotation of each joint in hand.

| Joint ID | J7 | J8 | J9 | J10 | J11 | J12 | J13 |
|---|---|---|---|---|---|---|---|
| Origin angle | 120 | 120 | 120 | 120 | 120 | 120 | 120 |
| Range of rotation | 64–192 | 80–160 | 120–224 | 32–128 | 53–128 | 120–184 | 120–149 |
| Corresponding part | Left shoulder | Right shoulder | Left arm | Right arm | Left leg | Right leg | Head |

### 3.2 Interactive Performance

During the interactive glove puppetry performance, the involved audience's movements and gestures are captured by Microsoft Kinect and then sent to the control system which is defined as a finite state machine. After judging these movements and gestures, control system computes the corresponding motions and send them to HinHRob. HinHRob carries out the corresponding motions with the actors cooperating with it.

In general, the place for the interactive glove puppetry performance consists of the performance area and the audience area which are connected by the control system. The layout of the performance place is shown in Fig. 3. Besides the stage of the performance area, there is a projection area which takes not only the shadows of the performance on the stage into the interactive performance, but also projection contents to create different visual effects. The performance

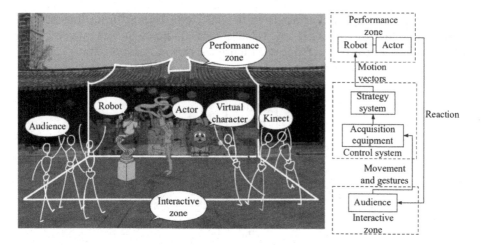

**Fig. 3.** The figure on the left is the layout of our interactive performance. The figure on the right describes the relations among all parts in the performance.

consists of three sections: prologue, repertoire and interaction section. For each section, different factors are considered to adjust HinHRob. For example, the robot needs to change its motion frequency based on the rhythm of the background music. Besides, the robot needs to change its motion so that it can face to the actors. Therefore, the strategy module is provided to make the robot react appropriately in different conditions.

**Strategy Module.** Robots motions can be a reaction to audience. This requires appropriate instructions to the robot in different situations. After the repertoire is decided, a finite state machine is designed in which each state controls a set of motions. For defining the state machine, the controlling motions of glove puppet are the first decomposited via analyzing the videos of glove puppetry performance given by the actors. And the key points of the controlling actions of the actors are then generalized into the finite states. As Fig. 1 shows, information including the movement, gestures and spatial information of the users captured by acquisition equipment decide current state of the state machine.

In performing section, actors' position is the most important information. After actors' position is captured, the strategy module computes the best motions for HinHRob, so that it can use appropriate movements and orientation to interact with actors. In crowd interaction section, audience's movements are captured and their movements can change the motions and direction of HinHRob. In interactive game section, the users' gestures are the major input to control the virtual character projected onto the background, and HinHRob can react and perform with the character.

For example, in interactive game section HinHRob is in idle state at the beginning. During this section, three kinds of gestures are to be recognized: fist, horizontal movement and rotation. In order to implement this function, the following spatial information needs to be collected: distance from fingertip to palm of each finger $d_1, d_2, d_3, d_4, d_5$, velocity of the palm $v_T$ and angular velocity of the normal vector of the palm $v_R$. Figure 4 shows an example state machine for the interactive game section.

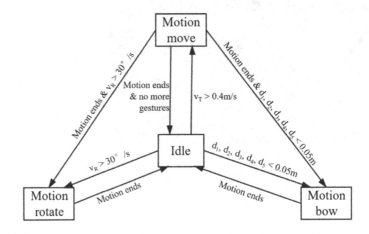

**Fig. 4.** A state machine used in the interactive game section.

**Motion Computation.** Robot motions are designed based on professional actors' motions. Each motion is divided into $N$ key frames, and a sub-motion vector $G_n$ is recorded in each key frame. Here $G_n$ is a thirteen-dimensional vector $(\omega_1, \omega_2, ..., \omega_{13})$, in which each $\omega$ represents the angle of rotation of each joint. $n$ means the $n$th key frame ($1 \leq n \leq N$). When a motion vector $G_n$ is sent to the robot, each joint of the robot rotates to the recorded angle at the recorded frequency as the vector indicates. After the robot finishes sub-motion $G_n$, the next motion vector $G_{n+1}$ is sent and performed until the complete motion is finished.

The strategy module computes motion vectors. IK algorithm is introduced to analyze these vectors, and two kinds of axial motion are extracted as the basic action of the system. The robot simulates human arm and has a simple skeletal structure, so the law of cosine is used to compute how many degrees each joint need to rotate. Figure 5 shows an arm with the upper arm length $L_1$ and lower arm length $L_2$.

Suppose that the target position of the arm is $(X, Y)$, then the upper arm needs to rotate with angle $\theta_1$ and the lower arm needs to rotate with angle $\theta_2$. As shown in Fig. 5, they can be computed as follows:

$$\theta_1 = arccos\left(\frac{L_1^2 + X^2 + Y^2 - L_2^2}{2L_1\sqrt{X^2 + Y^2}}\right) + \theta_T$$
$$\theta_2 = arccos\left(\frac{X^2 + Y^2 - L_1^2 - L_2^2}{2L_1 L_2}\right)$$

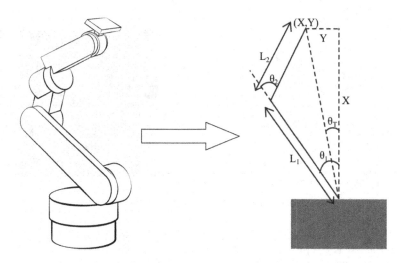

**Fig. 5.** Illustration of arm rotation.

Motions of arm and hand are independent to each other, but their frequency should be the same in the same motion so that they can be synchronized with each other.

## 4    Experience

### 4.1    Performance Configuration

Buzhengya square in Wudianshi traditional block, an ancient architectural buildings block was chosen as the place for the performance. The performance space design is shown in Fig. 6.

The performed repertoire is Daming Prefecture, a representative play in Jinjiang. A traditional Chou(joker) character was assigned to HinHRob because this character's funny motions are suitable for the robot.

### 4.2    Interaction Sections in the Performance

Interaction is an indispensable part in this interactive performance. Different modes of interaction are designed for audiences in three different sections: crowd interaction section, game section and finger dance sections.

In crowd interaction section, audience's movements are captured and the shadows of their movements and interactions are projected onto the background which is the cyan projection zone. At the same time, there are some virtual Hydrangeas on the virtual background, and audience's movements can influence Hydrangeas' movement as well as HinHRob's motions. Audience are firstly introduced into the performance to arouse the audiences' enthusiasm.

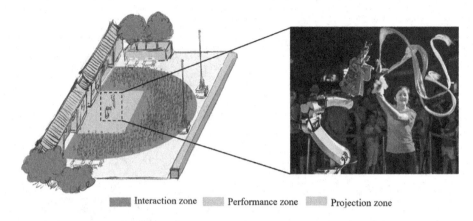

Interaction zone    Performance zone    Projection zone

**Fig. 6.** Prototype of the performance space and real scene of the performance. The figure on the left is the prototype of the performance space. The figure on the right is a photograph of performance stage.

In game section, there is a virtual character and some standard gesture examples on a screen. Gestures of a user are captured. If a user moves one hand horizontally, the virtual character moves correspondingly. The user can do different gestures and if a gesture captured fits the current example on the screen, the virtual character does a preset motion. At the same time, HinHRob gives corresponding reactions so that the user can perform with the robot. In this section, with a sense of control, the audience can be more immersed into the performance.

Finger dance is a dance with one hand. All the gestures in finger dance come from professional puppet-control gestures. When a finger dance starts, professional actors also join in the interaction with audiences. Meanwhile, HinHRob and the virtual character do the same motions. Here HinHRob becomes a bridge that connects audience and actors, which are segmented in traditional performances. All components of the interactive performance join in one finger dance, and audience's participation and immersion reach to the highest level in one performance.

### 4.3 Analysis

Real-time capability is the most significant for HinHRob. It influences the fluency of the interaction and user experience directly. Motion delay of HinHRob was tested and the average delay of HinHRob was less than 200 ms, which can be almost negligible to naked eyes.

As a kind of intangible cultural heritage, glove puppetry needs to be promoted among teenagers for its development. So after the performance, a questionnaire was delivered to 56 interviewees of a certain age. These interviewees' ages range from 10 to 14, 29 of them are boys and 27 of them are girls. Several questions were asked based on five properties: attractiveness, motions, improvement to performance, immersion and easy to use. Each question is a five-point scale question. The average score for each property is listed in Table 3. Figure 7 shows the score distribution of each question.

**Table 3.** Scores of each property of HinHRob in the performance.

| Property | Attractiveness | Motions | Improvement to performance | Immersion | Easy to use |
|---|---|---|---|---|---|
| Score | 4.66 | 4.38 | 4.23 | 4.15 | 3.80 |

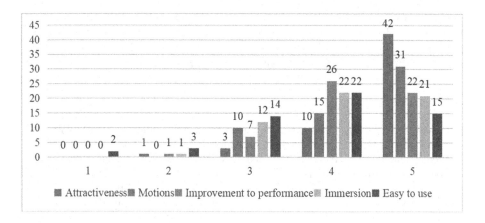

**Fig. 7.** Score distribution of each question.

The highest score is recorded in attractiveness, because as an emerging technology product in a traditional cultural performance, HinHRob can naturally arouse the curiosity of passers-by. Motions also gets a high score, that means HinHRob's performance in this repertoire indeed impressed audience. Most people thought participation of the robot is an improvement to traditional performance and they prefer a performance with robots than a traditional one. Apart from this, interacting with the robot can give more immersion to audience than watching a traditional performance. The property of easy to use only gets 3.80. There are many reasons for a relatively low score in easy to use, with most mention of the difficulty of the interaction games, and the low accuracy of acquisition equipments in the circumstances at that time.

The professional actors were also interviewed about the use of robot in the performance. They all approved with the novelty of using a robot into a traditional performance, and it could make it more easily accepted of the performance by audience. One of the interviewees said that the combine of traditional arts and modern techniques can attract the youth from a new point of view and give them a close quarters experience. However, there are still some shortage of HinHRob.

When asked for their evaluation of motions, actors were obviously more strict, and HinHRob got a 3.57 from 7 actors who had joined in the performance. 4 of these actors mentioned that the robot's motions needs to be improved. One said that our robot was still mechanical and it needed more flexible, varied and interesting motions to perform better.

## 5  Conclusion

In this paper, HinHRob is presented and used in an interactive glove peppery performance. The results show that HinHRob can be a connection between audiences and the stage, so that audiences can get a more immersive experience in the interactive performance compared with a traditional one.

There are still much future work to optimize HinHRob and the model of performance. Better motions will be adjusted for the robot, along with a more appropriate appearance. We would also like to design more kinds of interaction for both audience and actors to create a more immersive scene.

## References

1. Hansen, L.K., Rico, J., Jacucci, G., Brewster, S.A., Ashbrook, D.: Performative interaction in public space. In: CHI Extended Abstracts, pp. 49–52. ACM (2011)
2. Rico, J., Jacucci, G., Reeves, S., Hansen, L.K., Brewster, S.A.: Designing for performative interactions in public spaces. In: UbiComp (Adjunct Papers), ACM International Conference Proceeding Series, pp. 519–522. ACM (2010)
3. Benford, S., et al.: Can you see me now? ACM Trans. Comput.-Hum. Interact. **13**(1), 100–133 (2006)
4. Drozd, A., Bowers, J., Benford, S., Greenhalgh, C., Fraser, M.: Collaboratively improvising magic an approach to managing participation in an on-line drama. In: ECSCW, pp. 159–178. Kluwer (2001). https://doi.org/10.1007/0-306-48019-0_9
5. Way, D.L., Lau, W.K., Huang, T.Y.: Glove puppetry cloud theater through a virtual reality network. In: SIGGRAPH Posters, pp. 1–2. ACM (2019)
6. Lin, S.Y., Shie, C.K., Chen, S.C., Hung, Y.P.: Action recognition for human-marionette interaction. In: Proceedings of the 20th ACM International Conference on Multimedia, MM 2012, pp. 39–48. Association for Computing Machinery, New York, NY, USA (2012)
7. Valdivia y Alvarado, P., Youcef-Toumi, K.: Design of machines with compliant bodies for biomimetic locomotion in liquid environments. J. Dyn. Syst. Meas. Contr. **128**(1), 3–13 (2005)
8. Grizzle, J.W., Abba, G., Plestan, F.: Asymptotically stable walking for biped robots: analysis via systems with impulse effects. IEEE Trans. Autom. Control **46**(1), 51–64 (2001)
9. Chevallereau, C., Grizzle, J.W., Shih, C.-L.: Asymptotically stable walking of a five-link underactuated 3-D bipedal robot. IEEE Trans. Rob. **25**(1), 37–50 (2009)
10. Polyak, E.: Virtual impersonation using interactive glove puppets. In: SIGGRAPH ASIA Posters, p. 31. ACM (2012)
11. Liu, H., et al.: Hinhrob: a performance robot for glove puppetry. In: SIGGRAPH Asia 2019 Posters, SA 2019. Association for Computing Machinery New York, NY, USA (2019)

# Virtual Reality

# Efficient Metaballs-Based Collision Detection for VR Neurosurgery Simulation on GPU

Yang Shen[1], Huiwei Feng[2], Jian Su[2], and Junjun Pan[2,3(✉)]

[1] National Engineering Laboratory for Cyberlearning and Intelligent Technology, Beijing Normal University, Beijing, China
[2] State Key Laboratory of Virtual Reality Technology and Systems, Beihang University, Beijing, China
pan_junjun@buaa.edu.cn
[3] Peng Cheng Lab, Shenzhen, China

**Abstract.** This paper presents a novel hybrid model comprising both surface mesh and the metaballs which occupy organs' interior for the soft tissue modeling. Through the utility of metaballs, we are capable of simplifying the organ interior using a set of overlapping spheres with different radii. We first develop an adaptive approach based on Voronoi Diagram for the initialization of inner metaballs. Then, we resort to global optimization and devise an electrostatic attraction technique to drive the metaballs to best fill the space inside the organ's boundary. We simplify the surgical instrument as a collection of cylinders with different radii and orientation, and develop an adaptive collision detection method to facilitate the collision between the surgical instrument and metaballs. Our framework is built on the parallel computation architecture of CUDA, and thus can afford interactive performance on a commodity desktop. To illustrate the effectiveness, the above techniques have all been integrated into a VR-based ventriculoscopic surgery simulator.

**Keywords:** Collision detection · Metaballs · GPU · Neurosurgery

## 1 Introduction

The core research topics in virtual surgery include the physical modeling of soft tissues, collision detection and the simulation of surgical procedures. In virtual surgery, collision detection usually involves two types. One is the collision between rigid surgical tools and soft tissues. The other is the collision between soft tissues of organs. Currently, there are many existing collision detection approaches that can reach real-time interaction speed, which is around 30 frames

This research is supported in part by National Key R&D Program of China (No. 2017YFC0108104), China Postdoctoral Science Foundation (2019M660527), National Natural Science Foundation of China (NO. 61872020, 61977063, 61672149).

F. Tian et al. (Eds.): CASA 2020, CCIS 1300, pp. 43–50, 2020.
https://doi.org/10.1007/978-3-030-63426-1_5

per second (fps) [8]. However, in virtual surgery involving haptics, a much higher update rate at about 1000 fps is necessary to output stable force feedback [7]. Moreover, the physics-based computation, which contains complex deformation of soft tissues, is generally performed as a part of the collision response. Hence there is a significant demand on the efficiency of the collision detection algorithm for the entire simulation system.

In this paper, using metaballs, we present an efficient collision detection method in virtual surgery involving haptics. In particular, a novel hybrid model comprising both surface mesh and the inner metaballs is designed for soft tissues. The finer surface mesh with high-precision geometric structure and texture, is employed to represent the boundary structure of organs. Meanwhile, the interior structure of soft tissues is simplified by a number of coarse, overlapping spheres with different radii. The metaballs based organs could directly participate in collision detection and dynamic simulation. The simplified geometry of metaballs affords far fewer details for its interior structure. It could effectively reduce the computational cost during dynamic simulation. We also build the parallel computing architecture by CUDA at the system level. This framework has already been adapted to a VR-based ventriculoscopic surgery simulator.

## 2    Related Work

Our work involves two topics of computer graphics research. One is the collision detection. It can be handled by a number of approaches, which are usually classified into intersection tests and distance computation approaches. And a comprehensive survey for these techniques has been made in [4,11]. Bounding boxes intersection test is the most common approach in collision detection [2]. Triangle-triangle intersection test [5] is a popular and effective collision detection methods since most 3D polygonal models can be represented by triangle meshes. Distance computation is another useful way in collision detection [11]. Pan et al. [6] simplified the surgical instrument as a generalized cylinder-shaped object and presented an effective method to handle the collision between rigid surgical instrument and vertices.

The other related research topic is the metaballs generation and interactions. Bradshaw et al. extended Hubbard's theory [3] and proposed several easy-to-use methods to pack spheres in polygon mesh [1]. Weller et al. [13] proposed a fast collision detection method for solid objects by the inner sphere tree, which is constructed by a large number of non-overlapped spheres.

Generally, with the development of programmable Compute Unified Device Architecture (CUDA), parallel collision detection methods became accessible. Pazouki [10] used CUDA for parallel computing in collision detection and achieved a surprising speed-up.

# 3   Construction and Optimization of the Inner Metaballs

We present the framework of our method, which can be shown as Fig. 1. In this figure, the green block means this task is implemented by CUDA. The first stage is the inner metaballs construction.

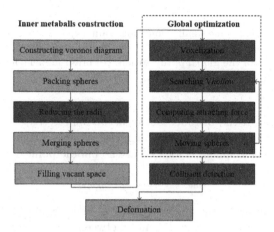

**Fig. 1.** The framework of our collision detection based on the metaballs. (Color figure online)

## 3.1   Initialization of the Inner Metaballs

In our technique, the first task is to fill an arbitrary object densely with a set of overlapping spheres and make the shape of metaballs best match the boundary of mesh. Besides, to reduce the computational cost during simulation, we expect the number of spheres could be as small as possible. Here we use Sphere Tree Construction Toolkit [1] to pack the spheres in organ mesh. However, the initial inner metaballs model after spheres packing hardly matches the mesh boundary very well. There are large parts of spheres outside the surface of the object. So a radius reduction process is necessary for the next step.

**Radius Reduction.** We calculate the shortest distance from the center of each sphere to the surface of the triangular mesh:

$$D(\mathbf{c}) = \min d(\mathbf{c}, \mathbf{Tri}_i),\tag{1}$$

This formula indicates the shortest distance between sphere center and triangle i. Then we adjust the sphere radius according to the distance $D(\mathbf{c})$, to ensure that the exterior parts of the sphere shrink inwards and contact with the surface boundary accurately. Figure 2(c) illustrates the result after radius reduction. In Fig. 2(c), we can find that small vacant space between spheres remain in some area. So next we will refine the metaballs model by a local optimization which involves spheres merge and vacant space filling.

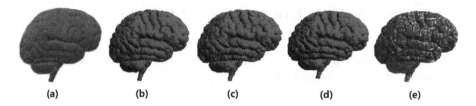

(a)          (b)          (c)          (d)          (e)

**Fig. 2.** The optimization of metaballs model for brain. (a) The triangular mesh of brain. (b) Initial inner metaballs model of brain after spheres packing. (c) Radius reduction result. (d) The result of the global optimization. (e) brain model contained both mesh and inner metaballs after optimization.

**Sphere Merging.** If the distance between two sphere centers is less than the radius of the smaller sphere, these two spheres will be merged into single one. The center of this new sphere is located at the middle point of the center line:

$$r_{new} = \min(r, D(\mathbf{c}_{new})), \tag{2}$$

where $r$ is the radius of the bigger sphere in the original spheres pair, and $D(\mathbf{c}_{new})$ represents the shortest distance between the new sphere center and mesh surface. Figure 3(a) shows an example of spheres merging.

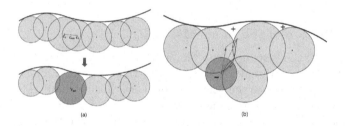

(a)                          (b)

**Fig. 3.** (a) The illustration of merging two extremely overlapping spheres. (b) The illustration of the electrostatic attraction model.

## 3.2    Global Optimization Using the Electrostatic Attraction Model

The ultimate aim of optimization is to make the shape of constructed inner metaballs best match with the boundary mesh. Here we voxelize the organ model at first. Then locate all the voxels which is not inside any sphere. We name this kind of voxel as $V_{hollow}$ and compute the sum of $V_{hollow}$. Our objective function of optimization can be expressed as (3):

$$\min sum(V_{hollow}), \tag{3}$$

Supposing each sphere can move freely in a local space inside the mesh and its radius is fixed. An electrostatic attraction model is proposed to solve this optimization problem (Fig. 3(b)). We treat each $V_{hollow}$ in this voxelized organ model as a unit "positive charge" and each sphere as the "negative charges". The quantity of "negative charges" is proportional to the volume of this sphere. To simplify the problem, we restrict each $V_{hollow}$ can only attract the spheres in its neighbouring space. The attracting force can be computed by Coulomb's law (Eq. (4)). Here $q_1$ is the quantity of "negative charges" which is proportional to the volume of the attracted sphere. $q_2$ is the quantity of "positive charge" for the hollow voxels near the attracted sphere. $k$ is a constant coefficient. $r$ is the distance between the attracted sphere and the center of hollow voxels. The resultant of attracting forces will drive each sphere move along its direction. We also implemented a number of kernel functions by CUDA for GPU acceleration.

$$F = k\frac{q_1 q_2}{r^2} \tag{4}$$

In each time step, we update the position of attracted spheres and $V_{hollow}$. If $sum(V_{hollow})$ decreases, save the current status of all spheres position. The iteration will end until $sum(V_{hollow})$ stop deceasing. The final distribution of spheres is the optimized inner metaballs model (Fig. 2(e)).

## 4   Collision Detection and Response

There are two types of collision detection in our surgery simulation system. One is the collision among multiple organs and self-collision of a single organ. The other is the collision between rigid surgical instrument and soft tissues.

### 4.1   Self and Multi-Organs' Collision

In ventriculoscopic surgery, there is frequent self-collision of soft tissue. The use of spheres in collision detection is not new and some similar approaches were implemented [10, 12]. Here we use a straightforward geometric projection method to handle the collision. It directly corrects the positions of spheres after a contact was detected. In this projection method, when intersection happens, a correction was directly applied to move the sphere to clear the occlusion. The direction of the movement is the normal of the intersection plane (Fig. 4). As there is no need to compute the penalty forces, the solving process can be speeded up.

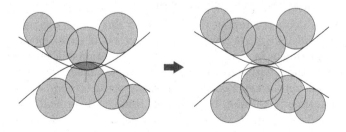

**Fig. 4.** Illustration of self-collision handling.

## 4.2  Adaptive Cylinder Based Collision Detection

Most interactions in virtual surgery happen at the collision and manipulation between surgical instruments and soft tissues. Therefore the collision detection of rigid surgical instrument and soft tissues takes the most computation time for interaction. In our virtual surgery system, as shown in Fig. 5, we treat the surgical instrument as the combination of a set of cylinders with different radii and orientations. An innovative adaptive cylinder based collision detection algorithm is designed. It computes the distance between each sphere and each cylinder to test whether there is a collision.

**Fig. 5.** The simplification of surgical instruments (abrasive drilling and rongeur) with a set of cylinders.

As the collision detection for each sphere and cylinder is independent, this algorithm is very suitable for parallel processing by GPU acceleration. We use each thread to compute the distance from each sphere to the tool respectively. If there is a distance less than zero, the intersection happens.

## 4.3  Collision Response and Deformation

In VR surgery system, after collision detection, the response and deformation of soft tissue is another important technical issue. Here we employed a hybrid physical modeling approach mentioned in [9] to deform the soft tissue. Then we treat the deformed metaballs as the "interior skeleton" and the triangular mesh as the "skin". An automatic skinning algorithm based on distance field is applied to map the deformation to the surface mesh in real time.

## 5  Experiments, Comparison, and Application

We have implemented our GPU collision detection technique by OpenGL, CUDA and OpenHaptics. All the experiments run on a desktop with NVIDIA GeForce GTX 1080, Intel(R) Core(TM)i7-6700 CPU (3.41 GHz) and 32 G RAM. The haptic rendering loop is running on a separate thread, so the update rate is guaranteed around 1 kHz. We have designed two sets of experiments.

The first experiment is to investigate the computation efficiency of our collision detection method, with and without GPU programming, for inner metaballs model in different resolution. Figure 6(a) illustrates the comparison of GPU and CPU execution time in collision between soft tissue and surgical instrument.

In the second experiment, we compare our adaptive cylinder based collision detection method with other two typical approaches [6,14]. Figure 6(b) illustrates the computation efficiency for them. Usually, the number of spheres in inner metaballs is much smaller than the number of vertices and faces in a mesh model. And when the number of vertices and faces increase, our adaptive metaballs construction method can maintain the number of spheres as a nearly constant in low level. Therefore our method is specially efficient to handle the collision of organs with large mesh data.

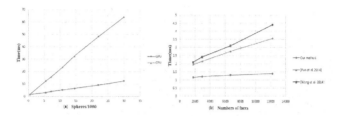

**Fig. 6.** (a) The comparison of computation time for collision detection between soft tissue and surgical instrument by our method (GPU vs CPU). (b) The comparison of computation efficiency for collision detection between soft tissue and surgical instrument among three different approaches.

Our ultimate goal is to apply our GPU-based collision detection method to the virtual reality based medical training. At present, we have incorporated it into a prototyped VR ventriculoscope surgery simulator (Fig. 7).

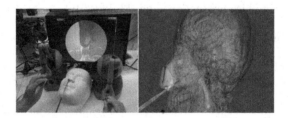

**Fig. 7.** Hardware and software interface of our developed VR based surgery simulator.

# 6    Conclusion and Discussion

In this paper we have presented a GPU-based collision detection method for virtual surgery using metaballs. It makes use of a hybrid model comprising both surface mesh and the metaballs. For the metaballs construction, we proposed an adaptive approach based on Voronoi Diagram for model initialization. For collision between surgical instrument and inner metaballs, we simplified the surgical instrument as a set of cylinders with different radii and orientations. And we employ CUDA to implement the adaptive collision detection method.

Nevertheless, our algorithm also has limits due to its special aim. It peforms well in blobby-like objects, such as organs, and rigid tools with generalized cylinder shape in surgery. The accuracy of collision detection could be deteriorated for objects with sharp features. Currently, we only implement the parallel computation for metaballs generation and collision detection. In future, we plan to further expand the parallel acceleration to the deformation with graph coloring.

# References

1. Bradshaw, G., Sullivan, C.: Adaptive medial-axis approximation for sphere-tree construction. ACM Trans. Graph. **23**(1), 1–26 (2004)
2. Gottschalk, S.: Separating axis theorem. Master's thesis, University of North Carolina at Chapel Hill (1996)
3. Hubbard, P.: Approximating polyhedra with spheres for time-critical collision detection. ACM Trans. Graph. **15**(3), 179–210 (1996)
4. Malukhin, K., Ehmann, K.: Mathematical modeling and virtual reality simulation of surgical tool interactions with soft tissue: A review and prospective **1**(2), 020802 (2018)
5. Muller, T.: A fast triangle-triangle intersection test. J. Graphics Tools **2**(2), 25–30 (1997)
6. Pan, J., et al.: Virtual reality training and assessment in laparoscopic rectum surgery. Int. J. Med. Robot. Comput. Assisted Surgery **11**(2), 194C–209 (2014)
7. Pan, J., et al.: Graphic and haptic simulation system for virtual laparoscopic rectum surgery. Int. J. Med. Robot. Comput. Assisted Surgery **7**(3), 304C–317 (2011)
8. Pan, J., Yan, S., Qin, H.: Interactive dissection of digital organs based on metaballs. In: Computer Graphics International, pp. 13–16 (2016)
9. Pan, J., Zhao, C., Zhao, X., Hao, A., Qin, H.: Metaballs-based physical modeling and deformation of organs for virtual surgery. The Visual Computer, 947–957 (2015). https://doi.org/10.1007/s00371-015-1106-y
10. Pazouki, A., Mazhar, H., Negrut, D.: Parallel collision detection of ellipsoids with applications in large scale multibody dynamics. Math. Comput. Simulation **82**(5), 879–894 (2012)
11. Teschner, M., et al.: Collision detection for deformable objects. In: State-of-the-Art Report, pp. 119–135. Eurographics Association (2004)
12. Wang, R., et al.: Variational sphere set approximation for solid objects. The Visual Comput. **22**(9–11), 612–621 (2006)
13. Weller, R., Zachmann, G.: A unified approach for physically-based simulations and haptic rendering. In: Proceedings of the 2009 ACM SIGGRAPH Symposium on Video Games, pp. 151–159. ACM (2009)
14. Wong, T.H., Leach, G., Zambetta, F.: An adaptive octree grid for gpu-based collision detection of deformable objects. The Visual Comput. **30**(6–8), 729–738 (2014)

# Posing 3D Characters in Virtual Reality Through In-the-Air Sketches

Alberto Cannavò[1]([⊠]) [iD], Congyi Zhang[2][iD], Wenping Wang[2][iD],
and Fabrizio Lamberti[1][iD]

[1] Politecnico di Torino, Turin, Italy
{alberto.cannavo,fabrizio.lamberti}@polito.it
[2] The University of Hong Kong, Pok Fu Lam, Hong Kong
cyzh@hku.hk, wenping@cs.hku.hk

**Abstract.** Generating computer animations is a very labor-intensive task, which requires animators to operate with sophisticated interfaces. Hence, researchers continuously experiment with alternative interaction paradigms that could possibly ease the above task. Among others, sketching represents a valid alternative to traditional interfaces since it can make interactions more expressive and intuitive; however, although the literature proposes several solutions leveraging sketch-based interfaces to solve different computer graphics challenges, generally they are not fully integrated in the computer animation pipeline. At the same time, Virtual Reality (VR), is becoming commonplace in many domains, and recently started to be recognized as capable to make it easier also the animators' job, by improving their spatial understanding of the animated scene and providing them with interfaces characterized by higher usability and effectiveness. Based on all of the above, this paper presents an add-on for a well-known animation suite that combines the advantages offered by a sketch-based interface and VR to let animators define poses and create virtual character animations in an immersive environment.

**Keywords:** 3D Animation · Sketch-based interfaces · Virtual reality

## 1 Introduction

Nowadays, the generation of virtual character animations is becoming fundamental for a number of applications, from the production of movies and videogames to the creation of a variety of virtual environments (VEs) used, e.g., in education, cultural heritage, product design, and social networking scenarios, to name a few [1,2]. However, animating 3D characters still represents a very labor-intensive task and is generally characterized by the involvement of expert users with significant skills in the field of computer animation [3,4].

According to [5], the complexity underlying the creation of animated characters lays in the posing step. In this step, animators are often requested to select and manipulate a large number of on-screen 3D "handles" for articulating the

© Springer Nature Switzerland AG 2020
F. Tian et al. (Eds.): CASA 2020, CCIS 1300, pp. 51–61, 2020.
https://doi.org/10.1007/978-3-030-63426-1_6

character's virtual skeleton. This set of handles is often referred to as an "armature" or a "rig", constituted by rigid elements named "bones". Handles/Bones can be used by the animators to directly or indirectly manipulate the degrees of freedom (DOFs) of all the individual character's parts/joints [6]. Unfortunately, many animation systems still leverage traditional interfaces for system input and output, like mouse and keyboard or 2D displays, which represent sub-optimal means to handle interactions encompassing a larger number of DOFs [3,7].

Considering the user input, among the approaches proposed in the literature to tackle the above issues a promising means is represented by sketch-based interfaces. It is worth mentioning that sketching is already exploited in others steps of the creative process, e.g., for building up shapes, exploring motion with rough key poses, drawing storyboards, etc. [8]. In fact, the literature shows that sketch-based interfaces have been successfully investigated by the research community to cope with limitations faced in various computer graphics applications, since they enable an expressive, simple and intuitive interaction that is close to the functioning of many cognitive processes [9]. Applications of sketch-based interfaces for character animation encompass modeling [10], rigging [11], posing [6], crowd simulation [12], etc. However, articulated characters may have a relatively high number of DOFs to control, and taking into account the complexity of operating with 3D elements through 2D devices or of interpreting 2D line drawings in 3D, it is not surprising that sketch-based animation of articulated characters remains an open problem [7,13].

For what it concerns system output, it is possible to notice that, similarly to the user input, it can be affected by the limited dimensionality of the visualization methods. With 2D displays, animators are requested to continuously change the position of the virtual camera or simultaneously look at multiple views of the scene been animated in order to visualize the contents of interest from the required viewpoint [14]. Both these solutions could led to an increased complexity in the usage of the animation tools, especially for novice users [3]. Given such limitations, an increasing number of users with different skills like, e.g., digital artists, filmmakers and storytellers, among others, recently started to pose their attention to the opportunities offered by Virtual Reality (VR) not only as a means to visualize character animations, but also to create them [15]. Although various commercial products and research prototypes are already available in the main VR stores, most of them provide a limited integration with common animation suites [3,16]. More specifically, in order to apply changes or reuse the animations generated within immersive environments, animators are generally requested to continuously perform import/export operations. These additional operations may slow down the whole animation process, and could be perceived as highly distracting by the animators.

By moving from the above considerations, this paper presents a system for character posing able to combine the benefits offered by sketch-based interfaces and VR technology. With this system, animators can manipulate a rigged virtual character by sketching lines into an immersive VE. To this aim, relevant works in the literature have been considered in order to extend the capabilities of existing 2D solutions to 3D immersive VEs. Moreover, the sketch-based interface is integrated in the well-know Blender modeling and animation suite[1], with the aim to let animators reuse articulated characters without the need for import/export operations. Lastly, since in the devised system the traditional and the sketch-based VR interfaces can be used at the same time, multiple users can observe and possibly work on the scene in a collaborative way.

## 2   Related Works

Researchers have long acknowledged the benefits brought by the use of sketch-based interfaces to execute a broad range of tasks in the computer animation field. For example, the authors of [17] presented a mathematical definition of the *Line of Action* (LOA), a conceptual tool used by cartoonists and illustrators to make the animated characters more consistent and dramatic. The system provides animators with an automatic procedure (based on an optimization problem) to align a 3D virtual character with a user-specified LOA. By considering this simple abstraction, the animator can easily adjust and refine the overall character's pose from a fixed viewpoint. The work proposes an automatic algorithm to define the correspondences between the LOA and a subset of the character's bones; the well-known *depth ambiguities* problem of 2D sketches [17] is addressed by constraining the transformations to the viewing plane.

In [6], a sketch-based posing system for 3D rigged characters was proposed letting animators create a custom *sketch abstraction*, i.e., a set of rigged curves that constitute an iconographic 2D representation of the character from a particular viewpoint, on top of a character's shape. When the animator provides a new input sketch, the system automatically tries to determine the rigging parameters that best align the character's sketch abstraction to the input sketch by minimizing the nonlinear iterative closest point energy. The distinguishing feature of the method presented in [6] is that it does not require any specific sketch representation a priori, but rather allows the animator to encode the sketch abstractions that are the most appropriate for the character to be deformed.

The work in [13] introduced a sketch-based character posing system which is more flexible than those introduced above. In fact, the sketches provided as input for character deformation may depict the skeleton of the character, its outline, or even a combination of the two elements. An optimization problem is formulated to determine the match between the subset of vertices of the character's mesh and the points obtained by sampling the input sketch.

The method that was presented in [18] is able to reconstruct the character's pose by using 2D "gesture drawings" and a 3D character rigged model as input. The benefit coming from the use of gesture drawings over other 2D inputs is the lack of perceptual ambiguities. Unlike stick-figures, LOA, and outer silhouettes, gesture drawings allow animators to unambiguously convey poses to human observers. By recognizing and leveraging the perceptual pose cues provided when creating these drawings, the system is able to automatically

---

[1] https://www.blender.org/.

reconstruct character's poses that are consistent with the animator's intent. The system is able to manage complex poses with varying and significant part foreshortening, occlusions, and drawing inaccuracies.

The work in [8] described a method to infer a 3D character's pose from a monocular 2D sketch. Since the devised method does not assume any specific characteristics of the model, it can be exploited with different types of characters. The 3D pose estimation is expressed as an optimization problem. In particular, a parallel variation of a Particle Swarm Optimization (PSO) algorithm [19] is used to manipulate the pose of a preexisting 3D model until a suitable pose is found. The pose is determined by automatically comparing the 3D rendering of the model and the input drawing. During the process, user's input is still needed to pinpoint the joints on the drawing.

## 3    Proposed System

From the analysis of the literature, it can be noticed that existing systems for posing 3D characters using sketches are still based on 2D devices. As a result, the viewpoint from which the sketch is drawn represents a key factor in the creation of the pose, since it influences the accuracy of the final 3D result.

The basic idea behind the system presented in this paper is to turn the existing methodology from 2D to 3D, letting animators draw sketches directly in an immersive VE. Figure 1 shows the expected usage of the proposed system. Given a 3D rigged character and some sketches drawn by the animator into the VE, the system is able to automatically align them by minimizing their distance. The system assumes that a skeleton is already defined for the character: hence rigging and skinning are not considered (both immersive and non-immersive methods reported, e.g., in [4] could be used to those purposes).

RIGGED CHARACTER              USER SKETCHES              3D POSE

**Fig. 1.** Expected use of the proposed system.

Another disadvantage of the solutions proposed in the literature is the fact that they generally come as standalone applications. Hence, integration with common animation suites like Blender, Autodesk Maya, etc. can take place only in a separate step of the animation workflow, thus making the process more tricky. The design reported in this paper considered the aspect above, and devised the system as an add-on for Blender. The aim of the proposed sketch-based system is not to replace Blender, but rather to offer an alternative interaction means that combines the affordances of posing characters via in-the-air sketches and the advanced functionalities targeted to character animation provided by traditional software, with the ultimate goal to speed up the overall process.

The steps followed in the development of the proposed system and the challenges to be solved can be summarized as follows:

- creating an immersive environment where the user can draw sketches;
- designing a methodology to find the best mapping between the sketches provided as input and the skeleton of the character to be deformed;
- developing a methodology to find the transformations to be applied to the bones in the character's skeleton in order to align them with the sketches;
- integrating the devised solution into a well-know animation suite

These requirements were considered in the design and implementation of the two main components of the system, i.e., a VR-based environment integrated in Blender letting animators draw 3D sketches, and a *matching & aligning* algorithm in charge of articulating the character's skeleton to make it assume the poses represented by the given sketches. In the following, more details about the VR-based environment as well as the functioning of the algorithm will be given. Current development state of the proposed system will be provided too.

### 3.1   VR-Based Environment for 3D Sketching

The devised system was developed as an add-on for Blender by leveraging two existing libraries: the Virtual Reality Viewport library[2] and the Pyopenvr SDK[3].

The Virtual Reality Viewport library lets Blender's users visualize a 3D scene (containing the characters to be animated and the sketches being created) into an immersive environment through a Head-Mounted Display (HMD). Pyopenvr is a binding for the Valve's OpenVR SDK designed to made the status of the HTC Vive's controllers (and HMD) available in Python; it can be exploited to implement specific functionalities when the user interacts with the controllers.

Figure 2 shows the main Blender's interface and the new add-on. On the left side, the window of *3D View* editor is shown, which contains the 3D objects, i.e., the virtual character (in gray), its skeleton (in green), the virtual representation of the two controllers (in black), and the sketches drawn by the user (in blue). The content of this window is visualized in VR through the HMD. The remaining panels are those of the traditional, mouse & keyboard-based, Blender's interface.

---

[2] VR Viewport: https://github.com/dfelinto/virtual_reality_viewport.
[3] Pyopenvr: https://github.com/cmbruns/pyopenvr.

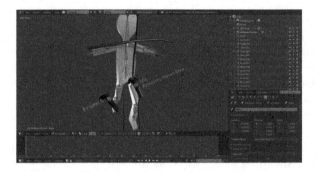

**Fig. 2.** Blender's interface and the new add-on for sketching in VR. (Color figure online)

The developed tool's functionalities can be accessed in the immersive environment by acting on the controllers. Currently, the tool allows the user to:

- draw a stroke (right controller's Trigger);
- select the character to pose (right/left controller's Gripper);
- apply translation and rotation transformations to the selected character (left controller's Trigger)
- launch the algorithm (right controller's Trackpad Up);
- reset the transformations applied to the skeleton by setting the rest pose for it (right controller's Trackpad Right);
- delete all the strokes drawn by the user (right controller's Trackpad Down);
- delete the last stroke drawn by the user (right controller's Trackpad Left);
- activate the playback of the animation (left controller's Trackpad Up);
- navigate the timeline by increasing/decreasing the current frame (left controller's Trackpad Right/Left);
- insert a keyframe to record the orientation of all the bones in the character's skeleton for the current frame (left controller's Trackpad Down)

Controllers' buttons functionalities are illustrated in Fig. 3. Visual feedback was introduced to simplify interaction with the system. In particular, on the right controller, a label indicates the current system's status, i.e., Idle (waiting for a new command) or Selection (functionalities for changing the skeleton to be manipulated available), and the currently skeleton selected. On the left controller, a label shows the current frame and the presence of a keyframe for the selected skeleton; if a keyframe has been set for the current frame, the text is colored yellow, otherwise it remains gray (convention used in Blender).

## 3.2    Matching and Aligning Algorithm

The devised algorithm represents a revised version of the method proposed in [13], where the problem of identifying the mapping between the pose of a virtual character and an input sketch was expressed as an optimization problem. The problem can be summarized as follows: given two sets of points, the sampled input sketch $Y = (y_1, y_2, ..., y_M)$ and a subset of points belonging to the character model $V = (v_1, v_2, ..., v_K)$, find the correspondence, or match matrix, $\omega$, and the amount of deformations in $p$ that minimize the energy $E_{3D}(\omega, p)$ expressed as:

$$min(\omega, p) \sum_{i=1}^{M} \sum_{k=1}^{K} \omega_{ki} \|y_i - v_k(p)\|_2^2 +$$
$$+\Phi(p) - \zeta \sum_{i=1}^{M} \sum_{k=1}^{K} \omega_{ki} \tag{1}$$

subject to the following constraints:

$$\sum_{i=1}^{M+1} \omega_{ki} = 1; \sum_{k=1}^{K+1} \omega_{ki} = 1; \omega_{ki} \in \{0, 1\} \tag{2}$$

where $\omega = \{\omega_{k,i}\}_{(K+1) \times (M+1)}$ is the correspondence matrix consisting of two parts: the upper-left $K \times M$ part defines the correspondence, whereas the extra $K + 1$-th row and $M + 1$-th column are introduced to handle the outliers; the points in $V$ and $Y$ having no correspondences are considered as outliers; $p$ is a vector containing the character posing parameters on the joints which deform points in $V$ to $Y$ in order to obtain a new pose $V(p)$ as close as possible to $Y$; $\Phi(p)$ is a regularization term, used to add further constraints for searching candidate solutions in a limited space; $\zeta$ is a scalar factor to weight the contribution of the last term of the equation, introduced to prevent treating too many points as outliers.

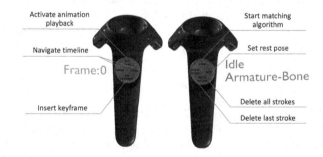

**Fig. 3.** Functionalities available through the controllers. (Color figure online)

In order to solve Eq. (1), the methodology presented in [13] proposes an alternating strategy to find the correspondence parameter $\omega$ and the deformation parameters $p$. Going back and forth between the correspondence and pose in an iterative way can help to solve the problem, since the knowledge of one element relatively makes it easier the determination of the other one.

By fixing $p$, it is possible to determine the sub-optimal values for $\omega$ by using two techniques: *softassign* [20] and *deterministic annealing* [21]. Unfortunately, in [13], no technical details were provided on how to use these two methods for the given problem. Hence, to implement them, the original paper presenting the use of these techniques for 2D and 3D point matching was considered [21]. The idea of the softassign algorithm is to relax the binary correspondence variable $\omega$ to be a continuous-valued matrix in the interval $[0, 1]$. The continuous nature of the matrix basically allows for fuzzy, partial matches between the two sets of points [21]. From an optimization point of view, this fuzziness makes the resulting energy function behave better, because the correspondences are able to improve gradually and continuously during the optimization, without jumping around in the space of binary permutation matrices (and outliers) [20]. The row and column constraints in Eq. (2) can be enforced via iterative row and column normalization of $\omega$ [22]. Deterministic annealing can be applied to directly control the fuzziness introduced with the softassign algorithm by adding an entropy term to the original assignment energy function in Eq. (1) [21]. The newly introduced parameter $\beta$ is called the temperature parameter. The name comes from the fact that, as one gradually reduces $\beta$, the energy function is minimized by a process similar to physical annealing. At higher temperatures, the entropy term forces the correspondence to be fuzzier. The values achieved at each temperature are adopted as initial conditions for the next stage as the temperature is lowered. According to the above techniques, the correspondence matrix is updated at each iteration using the expression $\omega_{ki} = \exp(\beta Q_{ki})$, where $Q_{ki} = -\frac{\partial E_{3D}}{\partial \omega_{jk}}$. At each iteration, the value of $\beta$ is incremented by a fixed amount which is defined at the beginning of the process.

Once the correspondence is found, it is possible to fix $\omega$ to obtain the parameters in $p$ which minimize the energy function in Eq. (1). Blender's functionalities were used to get the transformation values that best aligns the character's skeleton to the corresponding points in the sketch.

The algorithm is executed until the correspondence matrix converges or the maximum number of iterations is reached.

### 3.3   Current Development State

At present, the system supports multiple strokes and multiple skeletons; if the scene contains more than one character, all of them can be manipulated using the above approach (one at a time) by drawing a stroke for each of their bones. Figure 4 shows several characters (whose geometry was kept intentionally simple) characterized by armatures with a different topology. Figure 4a, 4e, and 4g shows the armatures in *rest pose* and the drawn sketches, whereas Fig. 4b, 4f, and 4h illustrate automatically computed poses. Figure 4c and Fig. 4d show a set of alternative keyframes that have been obtained for the armature in rest pose of the character in Fig. 4a by drawing the sketches represented in the figures. In order to show the current development state and the effect that drawn sketches have on the characters' poses, a video was recorded: the video, which is available

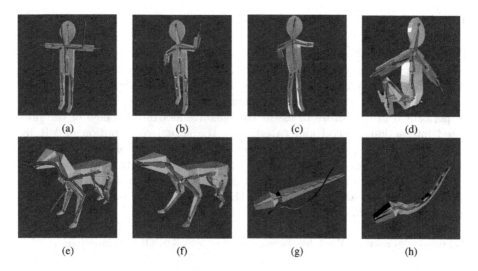

**Fig. 4.** Examples of armatures articulated through 3D sketches.

for download[4], shows a user animating two different characters. The source code of the project is available too[5].

Currently, the system presents the limitations reported below.

- The proposed algorithm assumes that strokes are provided for all the bones in the character's armature. If some strokes are not drawn, possible splits in the armature (e.g., the arms of the human character in Fig. 4a) will be mapped on the same stroke, by overlapping the two chains. A mechanism could be implemented to let the users specify the set of bones to be actually aligned, making the algorithm disregard some parts of the armature.
- Labels on the controllers representing available functionalities could be difficult to read in VR due to the limited resolution of the HMD. More meaningful graphics (e.g., 3D icons) could be used to improve the user experience.
- Users may find it difficult to accurately draw strokes in VR with the controllers, since visual feedback representing the actual position in which the strokes will be drawn is missing. Possible solutions could consider the integration of ad-hoc interaction devices (like, e.g., Logitech's VR Ink[6]) as well as methods to snap the strokes on given points.
- The high sampling rate of the controller movements could generate noisy sketches. Mechanisms could be introduced for sketch beautification.

---

[4] Video: https://bit.ly/35GdKqO.
[5] Source code: https://bit.ly/3eQPHK0.
[6] VR Ink: https://bit.ly/3ghpfcI.

## 4  Conclusions and Future Work

The proposal described above represents the baseline for a system able to perform a challenging computer graphics task, i.e., virtual character posing, by combining advantages brought by the use of sketch-based interfaces and VR technology. Besides tackling limitations mentioned above, experiments with end-users could be performed in the future to assess the effectiveness/intuitiveness of the proposed interaction method and to estimate the actual contribution of VR by collecting, e.g., the time required for posing different types of characters, data about users' tiredness, etc., possibly comparing it with traditional approaches. Moreover, effort could be devoted to integrating machine learning algorithms for making the system able to reconstruct the entire character pose or the overall animation by sketching only a few lines of the pose.

**Acknowledgements.** Work has been supported by VR@POLITO initiative.

## References

1. DiLorenzo, P.C.: Premo: dreamworks animation's new approach to animation. IEEE Comput. Graphics Appl. **35**(4), 14–21 (2015)
2. Lin, J., Igarashi, T., Mitani, J., Liao, M., He, Y.: A sketching interface for sitting pose design in the virtual environment. IEEE Trans. Visual Comput. Graphics **18**(11), 1979–1991 (2012)
3. Vogel, D., Lubos, P., Steinicke, F.: AnimationVR - interactive controller-based animating in virtual reality. In Proceedings 1st Workshop on Animation in Virtual and Augmented Environments, pp. 1–6. IEEE (2018)
4. Cannavò, A., Demartini, C., Morra, L., Lamberti, F.: Immersive virtual reality-based interfaces for character animation. IEEE Access **7**, 125463–125480 (2019)
5. Kytö, M., Dhinakaran, K., Martikainen, A., Hämäläinen, P.: Improving 3D character posing with a gestural interface. IEEE Comput. Graphics Appl. **37**(1), 70–78 (2015)
6. Hahn, F., et al. Sketch abstractions for character posing. In Proceedings of 14th ACM SIGGRAPH/Eurographics Symposium on Computer Animation, pp. 185–191 (2015)
7. Choi, B.: Sketch-based motion editing for articulated characters. ACM Trans. Graph. **35**(4), 146:1–146:12 (2016)
8. Gouvatsos, A., Xiao, Z., Marsden, N., Zhang, J.J.: Posing 3D models from drawings. Comput. Entertainment **15**(2), 2:1–2:14 (2017)
9. Annett, M., Anderson, F., Bischof, W.F., Gupta, A.: The pen is mightier: understanding stylus behaviour while inking on tablets. In Proceedings of Graphics Interface 2014, pp. 193–200. Canadian Information Processing Society (2014)
10. Li, C., Pan, H., Liu, Y., Tong, X., Sheffer, A., Wang, W.: Robust flow-guided neural prediction for sketch-based freeform surface modeling. In Proceedings of SIGGRAPH Asia 2018, p. 238. ACM (2018)
11. Borosán, P., Jin, M., DeCarlo, D., Gingold, Y., Nealen, A.: Rigmesh: automatic rigging for part-based shape modeling and deformation. ACM Trans. Graph. **31**(6), 1–9 (2012)

12. Mao, C., Qin, S.F., Wright, D.: Sketch-based virtual human modelling and animation. In Proceedings of 8th International Symposium on Smart Graphics, pp. 220–223 (2007)
13. Barbieri, S., Garau, N., Hu, W., Xiao, Z., Yang, X.: Enhancing character posing by a sketch-based interaction. In Proceedings of SIGGRAPH 2016 Posters, pp. 56:1–56:2 (2016)
14. Deering, M.F.: Holosketch: a virtual reality sketching/animation tool. ACM Trans. Comput. Hum. Interact. **2**(3), 220–238 (1995)
15. Gipson, J., et al.: VR Story production on Disney animation's cycles. In: ACM SIGGRAPH 2018 Talks, pp. 1–2 (2018)
16. Pantuwong, N.: A tangible interface for 3D character animation using augmented reality technology. In: Proceedings of 8th International Conference on Information Technology and Electrical Engineering, pp. 1–6. IEEE (2016)
17. Guay, M., Cani, M.-P., Ronfard, R.: The line of action: an intuitive interface for expressive character posing. ACM Trans. Graph. **32**, 1–8 (2013)
18. Bessmeltsev, M., Vining, N., Sheffer, A.: Gesture3d: posing 3D characters via gesture drawings. ACM Trans. Graph. **35**, 165:1–165:13 (2016)
19. Kennedy, J., Eberhart, R.: Particle swarm optimization. In Proceedings of International Conference on Neural Networks, pp. 1942–1948. IEEE (1995)
20. Yuille, A.L., Kosowsky, J.J.: Statistical physics algorithms that converge. Neural Comput. **6**(3), 341–356 (1994)
21. Gold, S., Rangarajan, A., Chien-Ping, L., Pappu, S., Mjolsness, E.: New algorithms for 2D and 3D point matching: pose estimation and correspondence. Pattern Recogn. **31**(8), 1019–1031 (1998)
22. Sinkhorn, R.: A relationship between arbitrary positive matrices and doubly stochastic matrices. Ann. of Math. Stat. **35**(2), 876–879 (1964)

# Evaluating the Need and Effect of an Audience in a Virtual Reality Presentation Training Tool

Diego Monteiro⬤, Hai-Ning Liang(✉)⬤, Hongji Li, Yu Fu, and Xian Wang

Xi'an Jiaotong-Liverpool University, Suzhou 15123, Jiangsu, China
haining.liang@xjtlu.edu.cn

**Abstract.** Public speaking is an essential skill in everyone's professional or academic career. Nevertheless, honing this skill is often tricky because training in front of a mirror does not give feedback or inspire the same anxiety as presenting in front of an audience. Further, most people do not always have access to the place where the presentation will happen. In this research, we developed a Virtual Reality (VR) environment to assist in improving people's presentation skills. Our system uses 3D scanned people to create more realistic scenarios. We conducted a study with twelve participants who had no prior experience with VR. We validated our virtual environment by analyzing whether it was preferred to no VR system and accepted regardless of the existence of a virtual audience. Our results show that users overwhelmingly prefer to use the VR system as a tool to help them improve their public speaking skills than training in an empty environment. However, the preference for an audience is mixed.

**Keywords:** Virtual Reality · Public speaking · Training · 3D scanned avatars

## 1 Introduction

The fear of public speaking is the most mentioned in surveys on fears [1]. Training for presentations can be challenging. However, in Virtual Reality (VR) environments, virtual characters can be used to train presenters to better meet their fears. Studies on the usefulness of a Virtual Audience (VA) for training people to make public presentations are limited, focusing mostly on phobic people [2, 3]. However, in many situations, other people would also like to practice interactive skills but lack the proper training environment, as is the case in language learning [4, 5].

It has been shown in previous studies that people, regardless of their fear of public speaking, present different heart rates when exposed to VA [6]. However, because this study was done with older technology, it is unclear if all people will be affected by a VA [7]. This is because even simple changes as the viewing perspective can affect VR interaction [8, 9].

Further, even though much research has been done to demonstrate that a VA can yield positive results in the treatment of phobic people [10–13], not as much has been done to see the usefulness of a VA for the general population. To this end, in this research, we developed a VR environment to enable users to make virtual public speaking activities or

© Springer Nature Switzerland AG 2020
F. Tian et al. (Eds.): CASA 2020, CCIS 1300, pp. 62–70, 2020.
https://doi.org/10.1007/978-3-030-63426-1_7

presentations. We ran an experiment to gather feedback from people doing presentations to evaluate the acceptance of our system as a training tool.

## 2 Related Work

Virtual Reality Exposure Therapies have shown potential, even before modern VR head-mounted displays (HMDs) [2, 11, 14, 15]. For instance, they have been shown to work well for different kinds of anxieties [3, 16], including public speaking [17]. Further, one of the most prominent uses of VR is for training [18]. Several studies have shown that VR is a disruptive and useful tool for the training of various skills [15, 19, 20], including technical [18], physical [21, 22], and sociological training [23]. Yet, realism is not always best [24], even low-end VR can yield positive results [25].

### 2.1 VR as a Presentation Environment

If conditions are adequate, VR can elicit similar presence levels compared to the real world in an interview setting [26]; it can even provoke fear [6]. Even though, these earlier models were not as realistic as what we can see in today's VR, people with social anxiety presented clear physical responses to them. However, these responses were not as prevalent in confident people. The reason for these responses may be because these participants thought the audience was not as realistic [6], or they ignored them like participants from a similar study reported in [27]. Recent improvements in the realism level might have changed this paradigm or caused social anxiety people to get so used to the technology that they do not get triggered anymore. Hence, this raises a question (RQ1): *What are people's opinions about VA made with the current technology?*

A newer study analyzed if a realistic environment could increase the presence in a virtual presentation environment [27]. The researchers from this study created a classroom identical to the one available in their environment. They then asked participants to present to a VA and asked a semi-structured interview. They observed that participants overall appreciated the experience, and some felt it becoming more real as they got accustomed to it. However, some stated not perceiving the audience even though they appreciated the experience. These responses raise our main research question (RQ2): *Is simply having a virtual classroom enough for (some) people?* To find the answer, we created a presentation environment in which participants could present either to a realistic empty room or to a partially 3D scanned VA.

## 3 The VR Presentation Environment

We developed a VR presentation environment to allow users to practice their presentations. We utilized pre-made models for the VA's body and movements. However, their heads were customizable 3D models of actual individuals; in our case the researchers (see Fig. 1). Based on the literature, we theorized that this would help the users feel more at ease before a real-life presentations [6, 27].

The VR environment contained a slide presentation on the back and footnotes in the front, which allowed users to present looking at the audience. The footnotes were akin to the presentation component in Microsoft PowerPoint; it let participants have notes in front of them (like a prompter). The audience always gazed at the presenter.

# 4    Experiment Design

To evaluate whether the VR audience was indeed useful and to validate our VR presentation environment as a tool to practice presentations, the experiment had three conditions. In one condition, the participants practiced in front of a virtual audience (VRP). In another condition, the practice happened in an empty virtual room (VRE). As the control participants also practiced in the room alone without VR (RLE).

We made a series of presentations in English with topics that the volunteers were not familiar with according to their backgrounds. The participants prepared within a specific time to become familiar with the topic, and then presented the slides to a real-life audience. For all these later presentations, there were always the same audience members. Since the participants could not see their virtual face, the face model was not altered (see Fig. 1); the participants' virtual hands matched their overall skin-tone.

**Fig. 1.** The faces of the audience and the prompter (left). The virtual reality presenter and environment (middle). One presentation in real-life (right).

## 4.1    Environment Metrics

Each participant was asked to complete a simple questionnaire to collect demographic data. All participants were asked to self-assess their English level among the 6 levels of the CEFR [26]. After, they completed the Personal Report of Confidence as a Speaker (PRCS) [28], which is a true-or-false questionnaire with a total of 12 points. The more the volunteer scored, the more anxious the volunteer was supposed to be.

We used the 5-Point Likert Self-Statements During Public Speaking (SSPS) [29], which is referred to as a marker for short term treatments. The higher the score, the more confident the presenter. Further, we asked the participants to rate from 0 (worst) to 5 (best) how good they felt the conditions were, and their familiarity with the topic.

After going through the three conditions, we asked participants to rank each version according to a list of criteria and to answer a few open-ended questions (see Table 1).

## 4.2    Apparatus

We used an Oculus Rift CV1 as our HMD, and two standard 27″ 4K monitors. We used the Oculus Touch to control the presentation (even the real-life presentation). Participants did not need to learn different controls for each version. We used monitors in real-life to simulate both the screen on the back and the text area facing the volunteer. All text sizes were set to be the same in VR and on the monitor.

Table 1. Open questions presented at the end of the experiment.

| ID | Question | Type |
|---|---|---|
| R1 | Rank your preparation after each version | Rank |
| R2 | Rank your nervousness after each version | Rank |
| R3 | Rank your version preference | Rank |
| Q1 | How do you feel about the virtual environment, not including the audience? | Open |
| Q2 | How do you feel regarding the virtual audience? | Open |
| Q3 | Is there anything you would change in the Virtual Environment? | Open |

### 4.3  Participants

We recruited a total of 12 participants (7 females; 4 males; 1 non-binary) from a local university. They had an average age of 19.88 (s.d. = 1.32), ranging between 19 and 23. No volunteer mentioned health issues, physical or otherwise. No participant was a native English speaker. Half had experience with VR systems before the experiment. The participants were not offered any reward to participate in the experiment.

### 4.4  Procedures

Each participant was assigned a specific order of the three conditions in which to practice the presentation. The order was Latin Square counterbalanced to mitigate carry-over effects. Participants were debriefed about the experiment.

Next, all participants were presented with a demonstration introduction of the Oculus Rift and a static virtual environment to get them acquainted with the VR HMD and set up—they were presented to the virtual room and a mock slide presentation.

Then, each participant was left alone to complete the training without being observed. The participants had 15 min to train for the presentation on the current condition. After this time, the participants were requested to remove the HMD and answer the questions. They then presented the topic in real-life.

The participants were given 30 min to rest before starting the next condition. After all conditions were tested, the last questionnaire was given to the participants. The participants were told that the open-ended questions could be answered in their native language if they felt more comfortable doing so. At the end, the participants were thanked for their time, offered time to rest, and some refreshments. On average, each volunteer took one and a half hours to finish the whole data collection process.

## 5  Results

The data were analyzed using both statistical inference methods and data visualizations. We conducted Mauchly's Test of Sphericity. We also employed Repeated Measures ANOVA (RM-ANOVA) using Bonferroni correction to detect significant main effects. If the assumption of sphericity was violated, we used the Greenhouse-Geisser correction to adjust the degrees of freedom. To control for both Type I and Type II errors we chose $p < 0.10$ for our analyses [30]. For the open-ended questions, we analyzed the sentences individually.

## 5.1 Pre-questionnaire

We defined the bins for PRCS, normally distributed, as between 0 and 4 as not so nervous, until 8 as regular nervousness. Anything above was considered as extremely nervous. We dubbed these bins as Group Not Anxious (NA), Standard Anxious (SA), and Extremely Anxious (EA), respectively. 50% of the EA participants declared their level as B2. The other volunteers were mainly self-declared as B1.

## 5.2 Questionnaires of Nervousness and Preference Order

The SSPS questionnaire revealed significant differences after having practiced in the virtual environment; the participants overall felt more positively to present to a real audience ($F_{2, 22} = 3.051$, $p = .068$). The positive effect was more present on the NA participants ($F_{2, 6} = 4.043$, $p = .077$). Post-hoc analysis showed that VRP was especially more successful (see Fig. 2) in making the participants feel less anxious ($p = .085$). The participants rated the VRP version the best as a training tool (see Fig. 2). However, EA participants did not rate it more positively as a training tool than the other versions. The main difference in ratings came from NA participants.

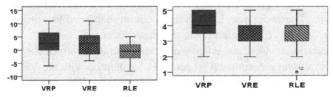

**Fig. 2.** SSPS answers after training in each version (left); VR versions scored slightly better. Participants' ratings for each condition as a training tool (right).

The overall ranking disregarding PRCS can be seen on Fig. 3. 75% of the EA participants chose one of the empty rooms as the version they felt most prepared in (R1). However, they all selected the VRP as their second option. All EA participants selected the VRP as the version in which they felt the most nervous (R2). Half chose as their first choice, and 50% preferred it as their second version (R3); only one EA participant chose VRE as their first choice. Overall, VRP was the condition that received the most positive overall feedback. Only one NA participant chose VRP as their first choice. The SA participants consistently chose it as their first choice.

## 5.3 Open-Ended Questions

The analysis of the interviews showed positive results and feedback. For Q1, one of the most common words reported by the volunteers is that the environment made them feel "good," and it was or felt "real".

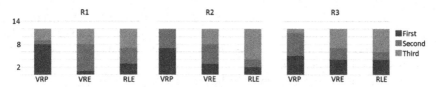

**Fig. 3.** Ranking to questions from R1 to R3, in their respective order from left to right.

Q2 and Q3 showed that participants believed that a virtual audience made them nervous, but they thought it was good. For example, P3 said "[I feel] a little bit nervous, especially when the audience's action changes." Some participants mentioned this as a positive point for making them better prepared to speak to the real audience later. P11 said that "There will be some tension, but it will then be easier in reality." P4 mentioned that the audience was good even though they made him feel "serious".

The EA participants were the ones who most used words such as "nervous" and "scared". However, those were also the ones who commented most positively about the use of the application. As P3, who scored the maximum in the PRCS, puts it, "[It] made me not so relaxed but really help me improve my presentation." In general, participants said that they did not want to change the audience.

### 5.4  Discussion

The answers to the open questions and the ranking suggest a preference for VRP, which also indicate that the use of this VR tool for training has the potential to be well-accepted, which is aligned with previous research [6, 27]. Further, the answers also show a positive aspect of having the faces of the real audience in the tool, which were described as having given them "good nervousness". Hence, the participants' opinion about a VA with the current technology (*RQ1*) is positive.

The rankings and the open-ended questions led us to believe that the fear factor generated by the virtual audience is favorable to the participants who, in return, trained harder, or started feeling more secure with themselves. This is expected based on the exposure therapy treatments found in the literature [6]. This might indicate that an even greater audience might bring even better results.

Overall, VRP was verbally declared the most popular tool for a training presentation environment. Thus, in most cases, it is valuable to have a virtual audience interacting with the presenter. However, some people are satisfied with training in an empty room, which answers positively to the *RQ2*.

Although most participants are content with the VRP version, we recommend adding a toggle button to satisfy users who might appreciate the VRE. Because the requirements for EA people seem to be different than that of those who just need to practice presentation.

## 6  Conclusion

In this paper we explored whether there is a need (and an effect) of a virtual audience in a presentation training scenario using Virtual Reality (VR). We did this analysis through a series of subjective metrics which indicate that even though most people do appreciate the virtual audience generated with the current technology, it makes them somewhat positively nervous. For some people, the current virtual audience is not necessary and are just as satisfied with the system without it.

Further, we observed that a simple audience that follows the users by looking at them is enough for creating a stimulating training environment for presentations in a VR environment. This is a system that aims to invoke feelings of anxiety and promote effective training. This VR environment was able to make users nervous and rated 4 out of 5 as an effective training tool. We observed that the development of a training tool for public speaking training is the most adequate when it can have an audience and users would preferred to have the option to it on and off, depending on their preferences. Overall, the results show that the tool we created seems able to help students.

**Acknowledgments.** We would like to thank the participants for their time. This research was partially funded by XJTLU Key Program Special Fund (KSF-A-03), XJTLU Teaching Development Fund (TDF-18/19-R17-115) and XJTLU Research Development Fund.

# References

1. Dwyer, K.K., Davidson, M.M.: Is public speaking really more feared than death? Commun. Res. Reports **29**, 99–107 (2012). https://doi.org/10.1080/08824096.2012.667772
2. Carl, E., et al.: Virtual reality exposure therapy for anxiety and related disorders: a meta-analysis of randomized controlled trials. J. Anxiety Disord. **61**, 27–36 (2019). https://doi.org/10.1016/j.janxdis.2018.08.003
3. Anderson, P., Rothbaum, B.O., Hodges, L.F.: Virtual reality exposure in the treatment of social anxiety. Cogn. Behav. Pract. **10**, 240–247 (2003). https://doi.org/10.1016/S1077-7229(03)80036-6
4. Cheng, A., Yang, L., Andersen, E.: Teaching language and culture through a virtual reality game. Chi. 541–549 (2017). https://doi.org/10.1145/3025453.3025857
5. Pack, A., Barrett, A., Liang, H.N., Monteiro, D.V.: University EAP students' perceptions of using a prototype virtual reality learning environment to learn writing structure. Int. J. Comput. Lang. Learn. Teach. **10**, 27–46 (2020). https://doi.org/10.4018/IJCALLT.2020010103
6. Slater, M., Pertaub, D.-P., Barker, C., Clark, D.M.: An experimental study on fear of public speaking using a virtual environment. CyberPsychol. Behav. **9**, 627–633 (2008). https://doi.org/10.1089/cpb.2006.9.627
7. Monteiro, D., Liang, H.N., Wang, J., Wang, L., Wang, X., Yue, Y.: Evaluating the effects of a cartoon-like character with emotions on users' behaviour within virtual reality environments. In: Proceedings - 2018 IEEE International Conference on Artificial Intelligence and Virtual Reality, AIVR 2018. pp. 229–236. IEEE (2019). https://doi.org/10.1109/AIVR.2018.00053
8. Monteiro, D., Liang, H.N., Abel, A., Bahaei, N., De Cassia Monteiro, R.: Evaluating engagement of virtual reality games based on first and third person perspective using EEG and subjective metrics. In: Proceedings - 2018 IEEE International Conference on Artificial Intelligence and Virtual Reality, AIVR 2018, pp. 53–60 (2019). https://doi.org/10.1109/AIVR.2018.00015
9. Monteiro, D., Liang, H.N., Xu, W., Brucker, M., Nanjappan, V., Yue, Y.: Evaluating enjoyment, presence, and emulator sickness in VR games based on first- and third- person viewing perspectives. Comput. Animat. Virtual Worlds. **29**, e1830 (2018). https://doi.org/10.1002/cav.1830

10. Slater, M., Pertaub, D.P., Steed, A.: Public speaking in virtual reality: facing an audience of avatars. IEEE Comput. Graph. Appl. **19**, 6–9 (1999). https://doi.org/10.1109/38.749116

11. Wallach, H.S., Safir, M.P., Bar-Zvi, M.: Virtual reality cognitive behavior therapy for public speaking anxiety: a randomized clinical trial. Behav. Modif. **33**, 314–338 (2009). https://doi.org/10.1177/0145445509331926

12. Poeschl, S., Doering, N.: Virtual training for fear of public speaking - design of an audience for immersive virtual environments. In: Proceedings - IEEE Virtual Real. 101–102 (2012). https://doi.org/10.1109/VR.2012.6180902

13. Poeschl, S.: Virtual reality training for public speaking-A QUEST-VR framework validation. Front. ICT. **4** (2017). https://doi.org/10.3389/fict.2017.00013

14. Côté, S., Bouchard, S.: Virtual reality exposure for phobias: a critical review. J. Cyber Ther. Rehabil. **1**, 75–92 (2008)

15. Harris, S.R., Kemmerling, R.L., North, M.M.: Brief virtual reality therapy for public speaking anxiety. Cyberpsychol. Behav. **5**, 543–550 (2002). https://doi.org/10.1089/109493102321018187

16. Cardoş, R.A.I., David, O.A., David, D.O.: Virtual reality exposure therapy in flight anxiety: a quantitative meta-analysis. Comput. Hum. Behav. **72**, 371–380 (2017). https://doi.org/10.1016/j.chb.2017.03.007

17. Zinzow, H.M., et al.: Virtual reality and cognitive-behavioral therapy for driving anxiety and aggression in veterans: a pilot study. Cogn. Behav. Pract. **25**, 296–309 (2018). https://doi.org/10.1016/j.cbpra.2017.09.002

18. Lee, H., et al.: Annotation vs. Virtual tutor: Comparative analysis on the effectiveness of visual instructions in immersive virtual reality. In: Proceedings - 2019 IEEE International Symposium on Mixed and Augmented Reality, ISMAR 2019, pp. 318–327 (2019). https://doi.org/10.1109/ISMAR.2019.00030

19. Psotka, J.: Educational games and virtual reality as disruptive technologies. Educ. Technol. Soc. **16**, 69–80 (2013)

20. Merchant, Z., Goetz, E.T., Cifuentes, L., Keeney-Kennicutt, W., Davis, T.J.: Effectiveness of virtual reality-based instruction on students' learning outcomes in K-12 and higher education: a meta-analysis. Comput. Educ. **70**, 29–40 (2014). https://doi.org/10.1016/j.compedu.2013.07.033

21. Xu, W., Monteiro, D., Liang, H.N., Hasan, K., Yu, Y., Fleming, C.: Assessing the effects of a full-body motion-based exergame in virtual reality. In: ACM International Conference Proceeding Series, pp. 1–6 (2019). https://doi.org/10.1145/3332169.3333574

22. Xu, W., Liang, H.-N., Zhang, Z., Baghaei, N.: Studying the effect of display type and viewing perspective on user experience in virtual reality exergames. Games Health J. **9**, 1–10 (2020). https://doi.org/10.1089/g4h.2019.0102

23. Chittaro, L., Buttussi, F.: Assessing knowledge retention of an immersive serious game vs. A traditional education method in aviation safety. IEEE Trans. Vis. Comput. Graph. **21**, 529–538 (2015). https://doi.org/10.1109/TVCG.2015.2391853

24. Makransky, G., Terkildsen, T.S., Mayer, R.E.: Adding immersive virtual reality to a science lab simulation causes more presence but less learning. Learn. Instr. **60**, 225–236 (2019). https://doi.org/10.1016/j.learninstruc.2017.12.007

25. North, M.M., Hill, J., Aikhuele, A.S., North, S.M.: Virtual reality training in aid of communication apprehension in classroom environments. Int. J. Emerg. Technol. Learn. **3**, 34–37 (2008)

26. Villani, D., Repetto, C., Cipresso, P., Riva, G.: May i experience more presence in doing the same thing in virtual reality than in reality? An answer from a simulated job interview. Interact. Comput. **24**, 265–272 (2012). https://doi.org/10.1016/j.intcom.2012.04.008

27. Gruber, A., Kaplan-Rakowski, R.: User experience of public speaking practice in virtual reality. In: Cognitive and Affective Perspectives on Immersive Technology, pp. 235–249 (2020). https://doi.org/10.4018/978-1-7998-3250-8.ch012

28. Hook, J.N., Smith, C.A., Valentiner, D.P.: A short-form of the personal report of confidence as a speaker. Pers. Individ. Dif. **44**, 1306–1313 (2008). https://doi.org/10.1016/j.paid.2007.11.021

29. Hofmann, S.G., DiBartolo, P.M.: An instrument to assess self-statements during public speaking: scale development and preliminary psychometric properties. Behav. Ther. **135**, 612–615 (2000)

30. Kim, J.H., Choi, I.: Choosing the level of significance: a decision-theoretic approach. Abacus. 1–45 (2019). https://doi.org/10.1111/abac.12172

# Image Processing and Computer Vision

# A Cascaded Approach for Keyframes Extraction from Videos

Yunhua Pei[1], Zhiyi Huang[1], Wenjie Yu[1], Meili Wang[1,2,3(✉)], and Xuequan Lu[4]

[1] College of Information Engineering,
Northwest A & F University, Xianyang, China
`wml@nwsuaf.edu.cn`
[2] Key Laboratory of Agricultural Internet of Things,
Ministry of Agriculture and Rural Affairs, Yangling 712100, Shaanxi, China
[3] Shaanxi Key Laboratory of Agricultural Information Perception
and Intelligent Service, Yangling 712100, China
[4] Deakin University,
221 Burwood Highway, Burwood, VIC 3125, Australia
`xuequan.lu@deakin.edu.au`
`https://cie.nwsuaf.edu.cn/szdw/fjs/2012110003/`
`http://www.xuequanlu.com/`

**Abstract.** Keyframes extraction, a fundamental problem in video processing and analysis, has remained a challenge to date. In this paper, we introduce a novel method to effectively extract keyframes of a video. It consists of four steps. At first, we generate initial clips for the classified frames, based on consistent content within a clip. Using empirical evidence, we design an adaptive window length for the frame difference processing which outputs the initial keyframes then. We further remove the frames with meaningless information (e.g., black screen) in initial clips and initial keyframes. To achieve satisfactory keyframes, we finally map the current keyframes to the space of current clips and optimize the keyframes based on similarity. Extensive experiments show that our method outperforms to state-of-the-art keyframe extraction techniques with an average of 96.84% on precision and 81.55% on $F_1$.

**Keywords:** Keyframe extraction · Frame difference · Image classification · Video retrieval

## 1 Introduction

Keyframes extraction, that is extracting keyframes from a video, is a fundamental problem in video processing and analysis. It has a lot of application fields like video coding, so it is important to design robust and effective keyframe extraction methods. Current methods are usually based on either pixel matrix or deep learning classification results [5,6,9,10,18,19]. However, they still suffer from some limitations. More specifically, the keyframe extraction techniques based on pixel matrix are not capable of achieving decent accuracies, for example, when

F. Tian et al. (Eds.): CASA 2020, CCIS 1300, pp. 73–81, 2020.
https://doi.org/10.1007/978-3-030-63426-1_8

handling news videos [16]. Nevertheless, the involved keyframes extraction could take a considerable amount of time [15].

Motivated by the above issues, we propose a novel keyframe extraction approach in this paper. Given an input video, we first turn it into frames and perform classification with available deep learning networks. The classified frames are split into initial clips, each of which has consistent content. We then design an adaptive window length for frame difference processing which takes the computed initial clips as input and outputs. Also, we remove the frames with meaningless information for previous results, such as black screen. Eventually, to obtain desired keyframes, we map the current keyframes to the space of the current clips and optimize the keyframes based on similarity.

Our method is simple yet effective. It is elegantly built on top of deep learning classification and the frame difference processing. Experiments validate our approach and demonstrate that it outperforms or is comparable to state-of-the-art keyframe extraction techniques. The main contributions of this paper are:

- a novel robust keyframe extraction approach that fits various types of videos;
- the design of the adaptive window length and the removal of meaningless frames;
- a mapping scheme and an optimization method on determining keyframes.

*Our source code will be released online.*

## 2   Related Work

Keyframes extraction has been studied extensively. We only review researches mostly relevant to our work. Please refer to [2,12] for a comprehensive review.

Some researchers introduced a keyframe extraction method for human motion capture data, through exploiting the sparseness and Riemannian manifold structure of human motion [17]. Guan et al. introduced two criteria, coverage and redundancy, based on keypoint matching, to solve the keyframe selection problem [3]. Kuanar et al. obtained keyframes with iterative edge pruning strategy using dynamic Delon Diagram for clustering [5]. Mehmood et al. used both viewer attention and aural attention to do the extraction [11].

Some researchers extract keyframes based on machine learning results. Yang et al. used an unsupervised clustering algorithm to first divide the frames, and then selected keyframes from the clustering candidates [18]. Yong et al. extracted keyframes by undergoing image segmentation, feature extraction and matching of image blocks, and the construction of a co-occurrence matrix of semantic labels [19]. Li et al. mapped the video data to a high-dimensional space and learnt a new representation which could reflect the representativeness of the frame [7].

Although Motion capture and machine learning are effective ways proved to extract high-quality keyframes through existing researches, there is still no one algorithm that can extract keyframes from these two perspectives at the same time and suit each kind of videos.

# 3 Method

## 3.1 Overview

Our keyframe extraction approach consists of four steps which are specifically:

1. Initial clips generation. We first obtain the classification results and split the classified frames into clips that respectively involve consistent content.
2. Adaptive Window Length for frame difference processing. We then design an adaptive window length for the frame difference method which takes the output of Step 1 as inputs and outputs the initial keyframes.
3. Meaningless frames removal. We refine the results of Step 1 and 2 by removing the frames with meaningless information (e.g., black screen).
4. Mapping and optimization. After removing meaningless frames, we finally map the current keyframes to the space of the current clips and perform keyframes optimization based on similarity, to achieve more representative keyframes.

## 3.2 Generating Initial Clips

ImageAI library [1] has four different deep learning networks (Resnet50, DenseNet-BC-121-32, Inception_v3, Squeezenet) separately trained on the imagenet-1000 dataset. The four networks in this paper are using default parameter settings, please reference [1] for more details. The classification softmax $(s_{i\,\max})$ is defined as

$$\text{softmax}\,(s_i) = \frac{e^{s_i}}{\sum_{i=1}^{N} e^{s_i}} (i = 1, \dots, N) \tag{1}$$

where $s_i$ represents the score of the input $x$ on the $i_{\text{th}}$ category. After the calculation, we take the maximum recognition probability of an image as its label.

We turn the videos into consecutive frames which act as the input to the networks. Since one object in different scenes involve different meaning, it is necessary to treat them as independent scenes. Based on the image classification results, we simply split each video into a few clips, each of which continuously represent certain content, by simply checking if the labels of the current and next frames are the same or not.

## 3.3 Adaptive Window Length

The original frame difference method [13] simply sets the window length to 1 or a fixed value, which is prone to generate undesired keyframes. To solve this issue, introduce a formula to enable an adaptive length ($L$) calculation.

$$L = \frac{\sum(frame)}{Exp\_value} \tag{2}$$

where $\sum(frame)$ is the total number of frames in the video, and $Exp\_value$ denotes the expected number of keyframes.

We will describe how we achieve an adaptive threshold in experiments (Sect. 4.1), based on the videos.

### 3.4  Meaningless Frames Removal

Some consecutive frames may deliver little information, for example, black or white or other fuzzy colors representing non-recognizable items. As such, it is necessary to refine the results in Sect. 3.2 and Sect. 3.3. We judge whether a frame image has information or not by defining as follows, where *mount* is the total number of different colors in a frame. The *mount* threshold (i.e., $T$) is empirically set to 600 after testing on a hundred randomly selected $640 \times 480$ pixels pure color imagines from the Internet and experiment videos.

$$P = \begin{cases} 1, mount \geq T \\ 0, \ others \end{cases} \tag{3}$$

### 3.5  Mapping and Optimization

To obtain satisfactory results and reduce redundant results, we propose to map the results by Sect. 3.3 onto the space of the results after Sect. 3.2. After mapping, we perform the first optimization by computing the average similarity of each frame in a clip, and one with the highest average similarity is set as the keyframe of this clip. Finally, if two keyframes of two consecutive clips that are generated in Sect. 3.2 have a similarity above 50%, we conduct a second optimization by simply choosing the first keyframe and discarding the second keyframe. This is because sometimes actual videos have fast switch of camera shots which leads to repeated or similar scenes.

Similar to [4], the similarity is formulated as:

$$sim(G, S) = \frac{1}{M} \sum_{i=1}^{M} \left( 1 - \frac{|g_i - s_i|}{Max(g_i - s_i)} \right) \tag{4}$$

where $G$ and $S$ are the values of the histogram after transforming the two images into regular images, respectively. $M$ is the total number of samples in the color space. More information can be referred to [14]. The expected keyframe is the one with the greatest similarity, as follows

$$\arg \max_k \left( \frac{1}{|C| - 1} \sum sim(G_k, S) \right), \tag{5}$$

where $(G_k, S)$ and $|C|$ are a pair of two frames (not identical) and the number of frames in the involved clip $C$, respectively. It is often not necessary to compare the similarity between frames of different clips due to the discontinuity and dissimilarity.

## 4  Experiments

### 4.1  Experimental Setup

*Data.* A dataset of ten videos are used to validate the proposed method, which includes six types of video (i.e., advertisement, documentary and games).

*Ground Truth.* Similar to previous research [7], three volunteers with multimedia expertise independently selected and merged the keyframes of each video. If some images deliver the same information, they are merged by manually selecting the most representative one and discarding others. Table 1 illustrates an example. We perform this operation on all the videos and the results are shown as MK in Table 2.

**Table 1.** Ground truth keyframes generation example.

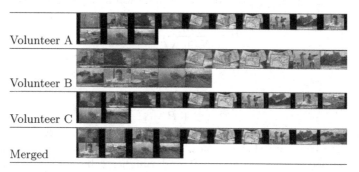

We display the numbers of keyframes for initial keyframes and final keyframes based on the four classification networks in Table 2. It can be seen from Table 2 that for each video, the numbers of final keyframes decreased in general, which indicates that Sect. 3.4 and Sect. 3.5 refine the initial keyframes. Our method runtime is also shown in Table 2 which sees 0.66–6.79 times of the length of the videos.

**Table 2.** Results and runtime by using different networks (in seconds). MK: merged keyframes. IK: initial keyframes. FK: final keyframes. RT: runtime R: Resnet50, D: DenseNet-BC-121-32, I: Inception_v3 S: Squeezenet. AVG: average

| Video | MK | $IK_R$ | $IK_D$ | $IK_I$ | $IK_S$ | $FK_R$ | $FK_D$ | $FK_I$ | $FK_S$ | $RT_R$ | $RT_D$ | $RT_I$ | $RT_S$ | $RT_{AVG}$ |
|---|---|---|---|---|---|---|---|---|---|---|---|---|---|---|
| Ads_Audi(84 s) | 22 | 29 | 31 | 17 | 21 | 21 | 22 | 17 | 18 | 368.1 | 442.9 | 295.5 | 208.0 | 328.6 |
| BBC...Camera(169 s) | 21 | 62 | 42 | 32 | 35 | 28 | 21 | 22 | 22 | 485.9 | 621.0 | 380.0 | 143.1 | 407.5 |
| Highlight_soccer(101 s) | 30 | 31 | 41 | 28 | 28 | 25 | 33 | 23 | 23 | 598.3 | 685.5 | 533.2 | 398.2 | 553.8 |
| lion vs zebra judo(18 s) | 3 | 64 | 55 | 64 | 100 | 3 | 2 | 2 | 2 | 88.7 | 104.2 | 81.4 | 37.9 | 78.0 |
| MV_Gnstyle(252 s) | 41 | 36 | 46 | 30 | 30 | 31 | 40 | 26 | 26 | 426.0 | 518.8 | 350.0 | 166.7 | 365.4 |
| Trailer...nonesub(161 s) | 46 | 37 | 23 | 30 | 26 | 18 | 15 | 18 | 16 | 284.5 | 315.8 | 225.5 | 115.3 | 235.3 |
| Trailer...sub(147 s) | 45 | 47 | 63 | 54 | 63 | 31 | 38 | 34 | 40 | 606.9 | 652.3 | 490.7 | 392.9 | 535.7 |
| Trailer_Pokemon(196 s) | 72 | 85 | 76 | 65 | 75 | 66 | 63 | 56 | 66 | 622.8 | 770.6 | 498.3 | 287.5 | 544.8 |
| UGS10_003(77 s) | 14 | 33 | 27 | 34 | 35 | 12 | 11 | 11 | 12 | 366.9 | 426.0 | 293.2 | 166.3 | 313.1 |
| Dragons Fight(87 s) | 10 | 27 | 25 | 27 | 27 | 6 | 7 | 9 | 8 | 270.1 | 316.7 | 234.8 | 128.1 | 237.4 |

*Experimental Setting.* Our framework is implemented in a Lenovo Y7000 laptop with an Intel(R) Core(TM) i5-9300H64 2.3 GHz CPU and a NVIDIA GeForce GTX 1050 Graphics card.

*Window Length.* We take the separated clips of ResNet50 as an example, to remove the short clips within a certain thresholding number. We found that the remaining clips by setting this threshold to 10 can cover 90% of frames from the whole video.

## 4.2   Quantitative Results

As with previous works [7,8,11], the precision $P$, the recall $R$ and the the average $(F_1)$ of the $P$ and $R$ are employed as the evaluation metrics. They are computed as:

$$P = \frac{N_c}{N_c + N_f} \times 100\% \tag{6}$$

$$R = \frac{N_c}{N_c + N_m} \times 100\% \tag{7}$$

$$F_1 = \frac{2 * R * P}{R + P} \times 100\% \tag{8}$$

where $N_c$ denotes the number of correctly extracted keyframes, and $N_f$ refers to the number of incorrect keyframes. $N_m$ is the number of missing keyframes. $F_1$ is a combined measure of $R$ and $P$, and a higher value indicates both higher $R$ and $P$.

Figure 1 shows the evaluation numbers for each video using four different networks, and we can observe that the accuracies of our method are high, except for only a few outliers (e.g., R network for V2 and V5). The average precision is 96.84%. Fig. 1(b) gives the recall numbers which are lower than precision numbers. We suspect that it has two reasons. The ground truth set of a video is simply removed high similarity frames. Moreover, some blurry frames can result in misclassifications and further lower numbers of keyframes. As a result, $N_c + N_m$ becomes large and $N_c$ becomes small, thus leading to relatively low recall numbers. Fig. 1(c) reflects that the overall performance is generally good, with an average of 81.55% for all videos and 84.69% for videos except the outlier video V7.

Besides the above experiments that validate our approach, we also compare our method with state-of-the-art keyframe extraction techniques [7,8,11]. Table 3 and 4 show some visual comparisons for our method and [7,8,11]. It can be seen from Table 3 that our extracted keyframes are very similar to current techniques [7,8]. Furthermore, our method can extract more representative keyframes, in terms of significant distinctions and front views. Table 4 shows that our method can extract fewer keyframes than [11] to describe the key content of the video. While the results by [11] seem a bit redundant, in terms of scene keyframes. Their scene keyframes occupied 36.4% while ours only took up 16.1%. This video is actually concentrated more on humans than pure scenes.

In addition to visual comparisons, we also conduct quantitative comparisons using the metrics mentioned above. The average $P$, $R$ and $F_1$ numbers are listed in Table 5. Our average $P$ numbers based on the four networks are the highest among all methods. Notice the numbers inside brackets are computed by excluding the outlier video V7.

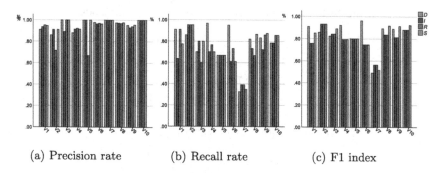

(a) Precision rate        (b) Recall rate        (c) F1 index

**Fig. 1.** Evaluation results. (a) Precision rate. (b) Recall rate. (c) F1 index. D: DenseNet-BC-121-32, I: Inception_v3, R: Resnet50, S: Squeezenet.

**Table 3.** Comparison with [7] and [8].

**Table 4.** Comparison with [11].

**Table 5.** Metrics comparison by using different methods.

|      | P             | R             | F1            |
|------|---------------|---------------|---------------|
| [7]  | 87.5%         | 84.0%         | 85.7%         |
| [8]  | 92.0%         | 87.8%         | 89.9%         |
| [11] | 90.0%         | 80.0%         | 84.7%         |
| R    | 92.8%(93.3%)  | 80.2%(79.3%)  | 86.0%(82.5%)  |
| D    | 93.9%(94.3%)  | 80.2%(85.3%)  | 86.5%(89.2%)  |
| I    | 93.5%(93.8%)  | 76.1%(74.3%)  | 83.9%(82.3%)  |
| S    | 95.7%(95.7%)  | 83.2%(80.4%)  | 89.0%(87.0%)  |

## 5    Conclusion

We have proposed a novel framework for extracting keyframes from videos. Various experiments demonstrate that our approach is effective, and better or comparable to state-of-the-art methods.

One limitation is that it is challenging to classify burred images for existing deep learning networks, thus leading to undesired keyframes for videos with frequent blur. As the future work, we would like to investigate and solve this limitation, for example, by incorporating deblurring techniques into our framework.

**Acknowledgement.** This work was partially funded by Key Laboratory of Agricultural Internet of Things, Ministry of Agriculture and Rural Affairs, Yangling, Shaanxi 712100, China ($2018AIOT - 09$). National Natural Science Foundation of China (61702433), Key Research and Development Program of Shaanxi Province ($2018NY - 127$).

## References

1. Open source Python library built to empower developers to build applications and systems with self-contained computer vision capabilities. https://github.com/OlafenwaMoses/frameAI
2. Asghar, M.N., Hussain, F., Manton, R.: Video indexing: a survey. Int. J. Comput. Inf. Technol. **3**(01), 1–22 (2014)
3. Guan, G., Wang, Z., Lu, S., Deng, J.D., Feng, D.D.: Keypoint-based keyframe selection. IEEE Trans. Circuits Syst. Video Technol. **23**(4), 729–734 (2013). https://doi.org/10.1109/TCSVT.2012.2214871
4. Jiang, L., Shen, G., Zhang, G.: An image retrieval algorithm based on HSV color segment histograms. Mech. Electr. Eng. Mag. **26**(11), 54–57 (2009)
5. Kuanar, S.K., Panda, R., Chowdhury, A.S.: Video key frame extraction through dynamic Delaunay clustering with a structural constraint. J. Vis. Commun. Image Represent. **24**(7), 1212–1227 (2013)
6. Kulhare, S., Sah, S., Pillai, S., Ptucha, R.: Key frame extraction for salient activity recognition. In: 2016 23rd International Conference on Pattern Recognition (ICPR), pp. 835–840. IEEE (2016)

7. Li, X., Zhao, B., Lu, X.: Key frame extraction in the summary space. IEEE Trans. Cybern. **48**(6), 1923–1934 (2017)
8. Liu, H., Li, T.: Key frame extraction based on improved frame blocks features and second extraction. In: 2015 12th International Conference on Fuzzy Systems and Knowledge Discovery (FSKD), pp. 1950–1955. IEEE (2015)
9. Liu, H., Meng, W., Liu, Z.: Key frame extraction of online video based on optimized frame difference. In: 2012 9th International Conference on Fuzzy Systems and Knowledge Discovery, pp. 1238–1242. IEEE (2012)
10. Luo, Y., Zhou, H., Tan, Q., Chen, X., Yun, M.: Key frame extraction of surveillance video based on moving object detection and image similarity. Pattern Recogn. Image Anal. **28**(2), 225–231 (2018). https://doi.org/10.1134/S1054661818020190
11. Mehmood, I., Sajjad, M., Rho, S., Baik, S.W.: Divide-and-conquer based summarization framework for extracting affective video content. Neurocomputing **174**, 393–403 (2016)
12. Asha Paul, M.K., Kavitha, J., Jansi Rani, P.A.: Key-frame extraction techniques: a review. Recent Pat. Comput. Sci. **11**(1), 3–16 (2018). https://doi.org/10.2174/2213275911666180719111118
13. Singla, N.: Motion detection based on frame difference method. Int. J. Inf. Comput. Technol. **4**(15), 1559–1565 (2014)
14. Swain, M.J., Ballard, D.H.: Indexing via color histograms. In: Sood, A.K., Wechsler, H. (eds.) Active Perception and Robot Vision. NATO ASI Series, vol. 83, pp. 261–273. Springer, Heidelberg (1992). https://doi.org/10.1007/978-3-642-77225-2_13
15. Tang, H., Zhou, J.: Method for extracting the key frame of various types video based on machine learning. Ind. Control Comput. **3**, 94–95 (2014)
16. Wang, S., Han, Y., Yadong, W.U., Zhang, S.: Video key frame extraction method based on image dominant color. J. Comput. Appl. **33**(9), 2631–2635 (2013)
17. Xia, G., Sun, H., Niu, X., Zhang, G., Feng, L.: Keyframe extraction for human motion capture data based on joint Kernel sparse representation. IEEE Trans. Ind. Electron. **64**(2), 1589–1599 (2016)
18. Yang, S., Lin, X.: Key frame extraction using unsupervised clustering based on a statistical model. Tsinghua Sci. Technol. **10**(2), 169–173 (2005)
19. Yong, S.P., Deng, J.D., Purvis, M.K.: Wildlife video key-frame extraction based on novelty detection in semantic context. Multimed. Tools Appl. **62**(2), 359–376 (2013). https://doi.org/10.1007/s11042-011-0902-2

# Extracting Highlights from a Badminton Video Combine Transfer Learning with Players' Velocity

Shu Tao[1], Jiankun Luo[1], Jing Shang[1], and Meili Wang[1,2,3(✉)]

[1] College of Information Engineering,
Northwest A & F University, Xianyang, China
wml@nwsuaf.edu.cn
[2] Key Laboratory of Agricultural Internet of Things,
Ministry of Agriculture and Rural Affairs, Yangling 712100, Shaanxi, China
[3] Shaanxi Key Laboratory of Agricultural Information Perception
and Intelligent Service, Yangling 712100, China

**Abstract.** We present a novel method for extracting highlights from a badminton video. Firstly, we classify the different views of badminton videos for video segmentation through building classification model based on transfer learning, and achieve high-precision with real-time segmentation. Secondly, based on object detection by the object detecting model YOLOv3, we locate players in a video segment and calculate the players' average velocity to extract highlights from a badminton video. Video segments with higher players' average velocity reflect the intense scenes of a badminton game, so we can regard them as highlights in a way. We extract highlights by sorting badminton video segments with higher players' average velocity, which make users save their time to enjoy the highlights of an entire video. We laterally evaluate the proposed method through verifying whether a segment has admitted objective details such as exciting response from audiences and positive evaluation from narrators.

**Keywords:** Badminton video · Views classification · Video segmentation · Average velocity · Highlights extraction · Key audio emotional

## 1 Introduction

Badminton videos are usually time-consuming, so it is necessary to select highlights to save video viewers time. In addition, professional users, such as players or coaches, have a great demand for statistics reasons of those video highlights. If a badminton video can be quickly analyzed and segmented, then special moment detections can be carried out instead of manual scrutinization of the whole games, and it can assist coaches to make better programs on players' training plans and game strategies [1]. To avoid expensive data streaming or excessively

© Springer Nature Switzerland AG 2020
F. Tian et al. (Eds.): CASA 2020, CCIS 1300, pp. 82–91, 2020.
https://doi.org/10.1007/978-3-030-63426-1_9

spending our time on watching games, users' preference for sports video shift from watching entire videos to highlights of videos. For example, watching the top-ten exciting or crucial of a badminton game directly corresponds to the video highlight extraction and abnormal scenario detection in sports videos.

Facing with the increasing amount of badminton videos and demanding user needs, badminton videos need to be effectively organized, expressed, managed and retrieved so that users can quickly obtain the useful information accordingly. To solve the problem, this paper proposes a method of badminton video analysis based on machine learning. The major contributions of this work lie in two aspects: (1) Segment a badminton video based on the classification of observation view; (2) Automatically extract the highlights from the video segments. Our work on badminton videos also provides a prototype of video analysis and can be easily extended to other types of sports videos in the future work.

## 2   Related Work

Many scholars have conducted interesting studies on sports video analysis and most of them concentrates on keyframe extraction [2,3]. However, the key frames extracted from the video cannot show the motion direction and trajectory of objects, which belong to the static critical messages in the video. Conversely, the highlights belong to the dynamic critical messages in the video and consist of several crucial clips of an entire video, which can satisfy users' demand of watching the dynamic critical demands of the video without manual processing.

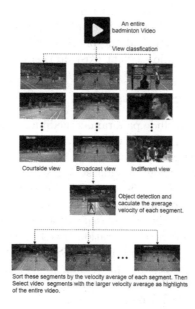

**Fig. 1.** The overall pipeline of our method.

This paper is different from those for keyframe extraction, and focuses on extracting highlights from an entire badminton video. Careelmont [4] proposed a method for the segmentation of badminton video and obtained the players' hitting strategies by extracting the moving objects from each frame in combination with the time dimension. In view of the highlights extraction, some methods extracted the highlights according to the user's different concerns and interest [5–8]. Sports video highlights can be interested on the basis of players' or referees' gestures and postures [9], and can be detected by the referee whistle sound [10], but these factors can not really reflect the popularity degree of a video. Fan et al. [11] employed real-time text stream, e.g.. opinion comments and posts, from social media to detect important events in live sports videos, but this method has some limitations because in many cases there are no comments or posts in sports videos. Yu et al. [12] proposed a method of perceiving audio emotional semantics and extracting video highlights extraction according to audio emotional semantics. However, the irrelevance of video scene leads to the low accuracy. In this paper, we extract highlights by calculating and sorting the overall velocity of both players in a badminton video, and through detecting key audio element [13] to evaluate the effectiveness of the proposed method.

## 3   The Proposed Method

Our proposed method consists of two parts. Firstly, the classification feasibility of three views in badminton videos is verified by the method of clustering, which establishes the classification model of views, so as to achieve the segmentation of badminton video. Secondly, we extract highlights of a video through calculating and sorting the overall velocity of both players. The overall pipeline of our method is illustrated in Fig. 1. And the predicted highlights are evaluated by checking whether the key audio element exist on them.

### 3.1   Badminton Video Segmentation

The views of soccer video include panoramic, medium, close-up and other views [13]. By observing and comparing, we can categorize the views of badminton videos as broadcast, courtside and indifferent view. See Fig. 2 for more details. The classification of views about broadcast and courtside are not affected by the background color or the specific view. But for the computer, it is difficult to understand the content of the image. Therefore, it is necessary to carry out pre-experiment to verify whether the classification of these views is reasonable. We verify the rationality of the classification based on the method of K-Means clustering [19]. Then we use the algorithm of t-SNE [20] to visualize the results of the status about pre-processing, processing by pre-training model and by the classification model MobileNet respectively, as shown in Fig. 3. And we can observe three views are better separated in Fig. 3(c).

Transfer learning can effectively solve the problem of insufficient data. In the multi-category tasks, the ImageNet dataset ISLVRC 2012 is often used, and it

(a) Broadcast view        (b) Courtside view        (c) Indifferent view

**Fig. 2.** View categories of badminton videos. Broadcast view and courtside view are the views of the camera overlooking the badminton court and looking at the front horizontal respectively, and indifferent view refers to others such as advertisements, game break, etc.

(a) Pre-processing        (b) Processed by pre-training (c) Processed by MobileNet
                          model

**Fig. 3.** The result comparing of the view classification. (a) The result before processing; (b) The result by the pre-training model; (c) The result by the classification model after pre-training. The red points, purple points and brown points represent the broadcast view, the courtside view, and the indifferent view respectively. (Color figure online)

includes a total of 1000 categories [21]. Before extracting the badminton highlights, the entire badminton video needs to be segmented into some useful segments relevant to the badminton game. The main view of useful video segments is broadcast view, which shows the action of badminton players in a game clearly and keeps the view for a long period. These video segments are the valid parts of the badminton videos, which laying the foundation for the highlight extraction. See Fig. 4 for the diagram of Segmenting a badminton video. The model of view classfication can effectively segment useful badminton video by transfer learning, which takes the model trained by ImageNet as the pre-training model. The main procedure of the badminton video segmentation is organized as follows. The following processing shall be done when each frame is input to the memory: If the view of the current frame is predicted to be broadcast and the previous frame is not broadcast, a storage queue is created for storing consecutive frames of the video segment which stores the current frame as the first frame. If both the current frame and its previous frame are predicted to be broadcast, the current frame is input to the latest created storage queue. Other cases are not dealt with. Finally, the storage queues amount is also the segments amount of an entire badminton video, and each storage queue corresponds to a storage space of each video segment.

**Table 1.** Training results of each network model.

| Pretraining network | Model size (Mb) | Accuracy of verification set | Loss of verification set | FPS |
|---|---|---|---|---|
| VGG16 [14] | 113 | 0.9836 | 0.0317 | 45.37 |
| ResNet50 [15] | 183 | 0.9770 | 0.0824 | 37.42 |
| InceptionV3 [16] | 168 | 0.9704 | 0.0729 | 36.58 |
| Xception [17] | 162 | 0.9770 | 0.0672 | 47.59 |
| MobileNet [18] | 26 | 0.9737 | 0.1071 | **52.31** |

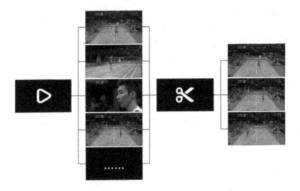

**Fig. 4.** Diagram of segmenting a badminton video.

## 3.2  Highlight Extraction

On the premise of maintaining the superiority of running speed, YOLOv3 [22] improve the detecting accuracy, especially strengthen the performance of recognize small objects. Thus we adopt YOLOv3 to detect players in a badminton video. In YOLOv3, the residual model Darknet-53 is used as the feature extractor, and realize multi-scale detection by FPN [23]. The detection result as shown in Fig. 5 (a). And Fig. 5 (b) shows the barycenter of players' object box, the top-left corner of a player object box is defined as $(x_1, y_1)$, and the bottom-right corner of the object box is defined as $(x_2, y_2)$, the barycenter of a player can be defined as Eq. 1. The target most likely to be a player may jump back and forth, thus it is necessary to consider all the players as a whole in each frame. The barycenter and velocity of the last player detected in two adjacent frames approximates the overall barycenter and overall velocity of all players. If we define the barycenter coordinates between $i$th frame and $(i + 1)$th frame are $(p_i, q_i)$, $(p_{i+1}, q_{i+1})$ respectively, then the overall velocity $v_{i,i+1}$ of the players between these two adjacent frames can be defined as Eq. 2.

$$barycenter = \left( \frac{x_1 + x_2}{2}, \frac{y_1 + 2y_2}{3} \right) \tag{1}$$

$$v_{i,i+1} = \sqrt{(p_{i+1} - p_i)^2 + (q_{i+1} - q_i)^2} \tag{2}$$

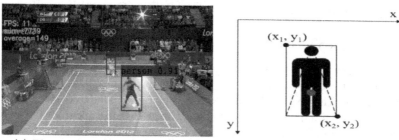

(a) Players detection by YOLOv3    (b) Barycenter of players' object box

**Fig. 5.** Players detection and barycenter diagram.

$$V = \sum_{i=1}^{N-1} \frac{v_{i,i+1}}{T} \tag{3}$$

Highlight extraction allows users to observe the highlights of the entire video directly. The higher average velocity of the players in a badminton video segment could indicate the higher intensity of the game, thus highlights of each video can be regarded as the segments with the higher velocity of the players. Through calculating the average velocity $V$ of each segment of broadcast view, the average velocity of a video segment $V$ can be defined as Eq. 3, where $N$ and $T$ are the frame amount and the duration of a video segment respectively. Then these segments are sorted to obtain the highlights.

**Table 2.** Location of badminton highlights. For example, the data "2-1:1" means the first highlight of the video "Thailand 2019" is located in the second game when the score of both players is 1:1. And "*None*" indicates the segments amount of the corresponding entire video is less than 10.

| Thailand 2019 | Malaysia 2019 | Indonesia 2019 | Spain 2019 | German 2019 | England 2019 |
|---|---|---|---|---|---|
| 2−1:1 | 1−15:6 | 1−0:2 | 2−8:8 | 2−15:11 | 2−3:2 |
| 2−19:13 | 2−2:3 | 1−3:9 | 2−8:11 | 1−2:0 | 1−16:19 |
| 2−15:11 | 2−2:1 | 1−2:5 | 1−7:14 | 2−20:16 | 1−5:10 |
| 1−0:0 | 2−3:4 | 1−2:7 | 2−2:3 | 1−12:6 | 2−7:8 |
| 1−2:2 | 2−19:19 | 1−3:10 | 2−1:2 | 2−8:8 | 2−14:16 |
| 2−20:17 | 1−6:1 | 1−0:1 | 2−0: 2 | 2−13:11 | 1−14:18 |
| 2−12:9 | 2−2:2 | 1−0:3 | 1−1:8 | 2−7:7 | 2−12:16 |
| 2−13:11 | 2−11:11 | 1−2:9 | 1−0:0 | 2−13:9 | 1−5:11 |
| 1−3:3 | 1−14:6 | *None* | 1−1:6 | 1−15:9 | 2−16:17 |
| 2−17:13 | 2−7:9 | *None* | 1−8:14 | 1−3:0 | 2−12:15 |

## 4      Experiment

### 4.1      Badminton Video Segmentation

This paper adopts the pre-trained image classification model with ImageNet [21], which improves the classification results and accelerates the convergence speed of network training. The results obtained by the pre-trained models of each network are shown in Table 1. The test indexes include the model size, accuracy of the verification set, the loss of verification set and FPS. Since motion video analysis pursues real-time performance, a faster computation speed is needed, and the model with highest FPS is MobileNet, which implements real-time computing and uses deep convolution instead of traditional 3D CNN [24], thus reducing redundant representation of convolution kernels [18]. Therefore, we take MobileNet as the basic network structure for deep learning. The main parameters of the experimental model are as follows: (1) The size of the input image is 224 × 224; (2) The dimension of the fully connected layer is 3, which correspond to the three views; (3) The image pixel value is scaled within the interval [0, 1] to prevent the influence of affine transformation and improve the computational efficiency of neural network; (4) The optimization of the network training is Stochastic Gradient Descent (SGD). We set learning rate 0.0001 and momentum 0.9. (5) The model serve for multi-classification task, thus we use classification cross entropy as the loss function, can be derived as Eq. 4, where $C$ is number of view classes, $p_i$ the groundtruth label concerning view class $i$, and $q_i$ the predict result of class $i$; (6) The batch size of the training data is set to 32. And the training strategies are as follows: (1) If the loss of the verification set does not decrease after 5 iterations, the learning rate is reduced by half. (2) If the verification set loss does not decrease after 30 training iterations, stop the training. The method described above yielded us an averaged accuracy of 95%, which can be considered adequate for the further tasks.

$$L = -\sum_{i=1}^{C} p_i \log(q_i) \tag{4}$$

We test six entire badminton videos[1] from YouTube to validate the effectiveness of the segments of them. In order to verify the generalization ability of the classfication model, the six videos in Table 2 are completely different from the training set[1].

### 4.2      Evaluation of Extracted Highlights

As Phomsoupha and Laffaye [25] pointed out, a scored shot usually takes from 7 s to 15 s. In this paper, it is believed that the segment whose average velocity is in the top $\varepsilon$ can be regarded as a highlight, where $\varepsilon$ is the threshold of average velocity rank, such as 10. Next, evaluating whether the extracted highlights are representative of the entire video.

---

[1] https://github.com/taoshu1996/BUILDINGTAO.

Li et al. [13] extracted the highlights of football games by detecting the key audio corresponded video clip from the football game – the excited voice of the commentators or the whistle of the referees. To make statistical results as objective as possible, we adopt this method to evaluate whether the extracted highlights is satisfying by judging whether they have response from the commentary or the audience, such as boo, shouts and warm applause in the extracted highlights. The time threshold set to 15 s in the experiments, and 10 video segments with the largest velocities average are used for verifications. The criterion of verification is the existence of some specific sounds, such as boo, shouts and warm applause from the audience or the response from the commentators during the stroke. The highlights of tested badminton videos are located by recording the status of the original game video and the score status of all the players. The scores of the players corresponds to the highlight are shown in Table 2. The statistics about the reactions from audience and the comments from commentators in highlights are shown in Table 3, which is carefully done by several badminton players. There are 58 highlights in 6 badminton games were extracted. Those extracted highlights which are marked with symbol "O" or "Δ" in Table 3 are considered as real highlights. In our experiments, 54 highlights[1] are evaluated to be true highlights, accounting for 93.10%, demonstrate the method in this paper is effective.

**Table 3.** Evaluation of badminton video highlights. The symbol "O" indicates that the highlight has a positive response from the audience, and "Δ" indicates that the highlight has a positive evaluation from the commentators.

| Thailand 2019 | Malaysia 2019 | Indonesia 2019 | Spain 2019 | German 2019 | England 2019 |
|---|---|---|---|---|---|
| OΔ | O | OΔ | Δ | OΔ | OΔ |
| OΔ | OΔ | OΔ | Δ | | OΔ |
| OΔ | OΔ | O | O | OΔ | O |
| O | OΔ | OΔ | O | O | Δ |
| OΔ | OΔ | OΔ | OΔ | | OΔ |
| OΔ | OΔ | OΔ | Δ | Δ | OΔ |
| O | OΔ | O | Δ | O | OΔ |
| Δ | OΔ | OΔ | | OΔ | O |
| OΔ | OΔ | None | | OΔ | OΔ |
| OΔ | OΔ | None | OΔ | OΔ | Δ |

## 5    Conclusions

This paper establishes a scene classification model through transfer learning in order to segment a badminton video for highlight extraction. We locate badminton players of each segment based on the model YOLOv3, and calculate the velocities average of all the players. We select segments of the high velocities as highlights.

Our work provides a prototype of extending the current model to other types of sports video highlight extraction. And we intend to build a statistical model through learning existing extracts by machine in the future work.

**Acknowledgement.** This work is partially funded by Key Laboratory of Agricultural Internet of Things, Ministry of Agriculture and Rural Affairs, China (2018AIOT-09), Key Research and Development Program of Shaanxi Province (2018NY-127), and supported by the Shaanxi Key Industrial Innovation Chain Project in Agricultural Domain (Grant No. 2019ZDLNY02-05).

# References

1. Li, S., Yang, X.: The overview of video summary technology. Technol. Innov. Appl. (2018)
2. Xia, G., Sun, H., Niu, X., Zhang, G., Feng, L.: Keyframe extraction for human motion capture data based on joint kernel sparse representation. IEEE Trans. Ind. Electron. **64**(2), 1589–1599 (2016)
3. Roberts, R., Lewis, J.P., Anjyo, K., Seo, J., Seol, Y.: Optimal and interactive keyframe selection for motion capture. Comput. Vis. Media (2019)
4. Careelmont, S.: Badminton shot classification in compressed video with baseline angled camera. Master's thesis [Academic thesis] (2013)
5. Bu, Q., Hu, A.: An approach to user-oriented highlights extraction from a sport video, vol. 21. College of Information Science and Engineering (2008)
6. Huang, Q., Zheng, Y., Jiang, S., Gao, W.: User attention analysis based video summarization and highlight ranking. Chin. J. Comput. **31**, 1612–1621 (2008)
7. Chakraborty, P.R., Tjondronegoro, D., Zhang, L., Chandran, V.: Automatic identification of sports video highlights using viewer interest features. In: Proceedings of the 2016 ACM on International Conference on Multimedia Retrieval (2016)
8. Wang, H., Huangyue, Yu., Hua, R., Zou, L.: Video highlight extraction based on the interests of users. J. Image Graph. **23**(5), 0748–0755 (2018)
9. Choroś, K.: Highlights extraction in sports videos based on automatic posture and gesture recognition. In: Nguyen, N.T., Tojo, S., Nguyen, L.M., Trawiński, B. (eds.) ACIIDS 2017. LNCS (LNAI), vol. 10191, pp. 619–628. Springer, Cham (2017). https://doi.org/10.1007/978-3-319-54472-4_58
10. Kathirvel, P., Manikandan, M.S., Soman, K.P.: Automated referee whistle sound detection for extraction of highlights from sports video. Int. J. Comput. Appl. **12**(11), 16–21 (2011)
11. Fan, Y.-C., Chen, H., Chen, W.-A.: A framework for extracting sports video highlights using social media. In: Ho, Y.-S., Sang, J., Ro, Y.M., Kim, J., Wu, F. (eds.) PCM 2015. LNCS, vol. 9315, pp. 670–677. Springer, Cham (2015). https://doi.org/10.1007/978-3-319-24078-7_69
12. Yu, C., Weng, Z.: Audio emotion perception and video highlight extraction, vol. 27. College of Mathematics and Computer Science (2015)
13. Li, J., Wang, T., Hu, W., Sun, M., Zhang, Y.: Soccer highlight detection using two-dependence Bayesian network. In: IEEE International Conference on Multimedia & Expo (2006)
14. Simonyan, K., Zisserman, A.: Very deep convolutional networks for large-scale image recognition, vol. 09 (2014)

15. He, K., Zhang, X., Ren, S., Sun, J.: Deep residual learning for image recognition. In: IEEE Conference on Computer Vision and Pattern Recognition (CVPR), pp. 770–778, June 2016
16. Szegedy, C., Vanhoucke, V., Ioffe, S., Shlens, J., Wojna, Z.: Rethinking the inception architecture for computer vision. In: CVPR, pp. 2818–2826, June 2016
17. Chollet, F.: Xception: deep learning with depthwise separable convolutions. In: Computer Vision and Pattern Recognition (CVPR), pp. 1800–1807, July 2017
18. Howard, A.: MobileNets: efficient convolutional neural networks for mobile vision applications. In: Computer Vision and Pattern Recognition (CVPR), April 2017
19. Coates, A., Ng, A.Y.: Learning feature representations with k-means. In: Montavon, G., Orr, G.B., Müller, K.-R. (eds.) Neural Networks: Tricks of the Trade. LNCS, vol. 7700, pp. 561–580. Springer, Heidelberg (2012). https://doi.org/10.1007/978-3-642-35289-8_30
20. Laurens, V.D.M., Hinton, G.: Visualizing data using t-SNE. J. Mach. Learn. Res. 9(2605), 2579–2605 (2008)
21. Russakovsky, O., et al.: ImageNet large scale visual recognition challenge. Int. J. Comput. Vis. 115(3), 211–252 (2015). https://doi.org/10.1007/s11263-015-0816-y
22. Redmon, J., Farhadi, A.: YOLOv3: an incremental improvement. CoRR, abs/1804.02767 (2018)
23. Lin, T.-Y., Dollár, P., Girshick, R., He, K., Hariharan, B.: Feature pyramid networks for object detection (2016)
24. Tran, D., Bourdev, L.D., Fergus, R., Torresani, L., Paluri, M.: Learning spatiotemporal features with 3D convolutional networks. CoRR, abs/1412.0767 (2014)
25. Phomsoupha, M., Laffaye, G.: The science of badminton: game characteristics, anthropometry, physiology, visual fitness and biomechanics. Sports Med. 45(4), 473–495 (2015). https://doi.org/10.1007/s40279-014-0287-2

# Dynamic Human Body Size Measurement Based on Feature Points Prediction and Mapping

Xiaohui Tan[1], Zhengyuan Lv[1], Kang Wang[2(✉)], and Xiaosong Yang[3]

[1] College of Information and Engineering, Capital Normal University,
Beijing 100048, China
[2] College of Management, Capital Normal University,
Beijing 100048, China
aaron_cnu@163.com
[3] Bournemouth University, Bournemouth, UK

**Abstract.** In this paper, we tackle the problem of measuring the sizes in different 3D human body motion models. We consider the problem of unexpected sizes when customers buy clothes in online shops because of past static dimensions measurement cannot meet dynamic requirements. The main contribution is a method that helps customers buy suitable clothes with a depth camera at home. Firstly, a random forest regression model is used to get the location of semantic feature points. Secondly, the tracking results are calculated with the help of a function map method which maps the semantic feature points between source model and motion sequence. Finally, we can calculate sizes of motion models with semantic feature points, with which can help evaluate whether a specific clothing is fit to body when doing actions. The proposed method accepts automatically predicting the points on 3D human models with scale transformation and even partial loss. A wide variety of experiments are conducted in which the method proved to achieve a significant result for anthropometric measurement in motion.

**Keywords:** Anthropometric measurement · Random forest · Mapping

## Introduction

Virtual fitting has received extensive attention with the development of electronic commerce. One can get suitable clothes with online shopping software. Despite its great advantages, online shopping also faces challenging tasks. Customers face the problems of unexpected sizes when they make different actions

This work was supported in part by the National Key R&D Program of China (2017YFB1002804), in part by the National Natural Science Foundation of China (61602324), in part by the Open Project of State Key Lab of CAD & CG, Zhejiang University (A1914), in part by the Beijing Natural Science Foundation (4194072).

© Springer Nature Switzerland AG 2020
F. Tian et al. (Eds.): CASA 2020, CCIS 1300, pp. 92–100, 2020.
https://doi.org/10.1007/978-3-030-63426-1_10

because of existing techniques are based on static measurements and limited to 2D images which makes it unsuitable for widely application [12].

Traditional virtual fitting method includes two main steps: 3D human body reconstruction and cloth simulation. They always reconstruct 3D human body through 2D images, 3D scans or 4D scans which suffer the problems of massive computations and expensive scanning device [3–5,11]. In recent work [10], it uses a 4D camera system to scan the way clothing moves on a body but the complicated camera system can't be cheap.

We propose a novel method that can help customers buy suitable clothes online with a depth camera which can easily work at home. The method consists of five parts, the detailed steps are shown in Fig. 1 and described as follows:

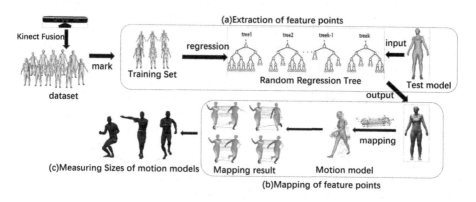

**Fig. 1.** Work flow

- Step 1: We use the method proposed in [7] to reconstruct 3D human body model, and use the model to generate different motion sequences with the method in [1].
- Step 2: We define 28 semantic feature points based on the standards of apparel industry [6] and mark the landmarks on sampling model set by hand as illustrated in Fig. 1(a). It is our training set which is used in training the random forest regression model. With the training set, we train the random forest regression model which can predict the location of the feature points on a new model shown in Fig. 1(a).
- Step 3: Using the motion sequence, with the function mapping method, we track the points from source model to motion model (a frame in motion sequences). As shown in Fig. 1(b), we can finally get the correspondence of feature points between template model and motion models.
- Step 4: According to the position of feature points, we measure the sizes of template model and motion models, and determine whether the clothes are fitted according to the changes of size.

# 1   Method

## 1.1   Random Forest Regression Analysis

We use random forest regression models to get the location of predefined points, which is proposed in [14]. The method contains two steps: training and testing. In the training process, some points need to be sampled from the training set firstly, and then the feature descriptors of sampling points and geodesic distance (to the predefined feature points) are calculated. A random forest regression model is trained by building a number of regression trees, each one is built recursively by split feature set and the process will end when the size of node meets the threshold value. The trained model maps the feature descriptor of sample points to geodesic distance. In the testing process, a number of points are sampled, and their feature descriptors are calculated at the same time. Given the descriptors of sampling points, the regression model will predict a distance to the desired point. Then each tree will give a distance and the model will use the mathematical expectation of all distances as the predict result. Using the distances, we can locate the feature points with a method like GPS which can help reduce the predicting points to a certain range. Then we use a voting strategy to locate the feature points. We give less weight to the points away from the feature point, and more weight to the points near the feature point.

In previous work [14], the parameters are set by experience and the value of each parameter is set separately. It ignored the interplay between computation time cost and error rate. Some parameters take a lot of time but bring little reduction of the error. We propose a method to solve the problem. Firstly, a mean square error objective function is defined as the following:

$$E = \lambda_{tr} E_{tree\_n} + \lambda_{no} E_{node\_s} + \lambda_{spr} E_{sample\_r} + \lambda_{sn} E_{shape\_n} \tag{1}$$

where $E$ is used to measure the quality of the training model, $E_{tree\_n}$ is the number of training model trees, $E_{node\_s}$ represents the size of leaf node, $E_{sample\_r}$ is the sampling rate of the model, $E_{shape\_n}$ is the number of training model and $\lambda$ is the impact factor of each $E_X$ (we use $E_X$ to represent $E_{tree\_n}$, $E_{node\_s}$, $E_{sample\_r}$ or $E_{shape\_n}$). $\lambda$ is defined as the mean square error per unit time, for example, $\lambda_{tr}$ is defined as the following:

$$\lambda_{tr} = \left| \frac{E_{var}}{t_{var}} \right| \tag{2}$$

where $E_{var}$ and $t_{var}$ represent the variation of mean square error and the time variation when $E_{tree\_n}$ changes, respectively. $\lambda_{tr}$ evaluate the error and the computation time cost simultaneously. As a result, the value of $\lambda$ represents the contribution to $E_X$ that can be of help to decide which parameter is more valuable. It means we need to compare the value of $\lambda$, the biggest one among them means the maximal contribution to $E$. A method is proposed to compare the value of $\lambda$ and set the value of $E_X$. The method consists of the following three steps:

- Step 1. Get a proper value of $E_X$ when there is no significant decline in error when time changes.
- Step 2. Calculate the value of $\lambda$ based on the value of $E_X$ in step 1.
- Step 3. Increase the values of $\lambda$ which have more contribution to the value of $E_X$ while decrease the values of $\lambda$ which have little effect on $E_X$.

## 1.2   3D Human Body Mapping

Our 3D shape correspondence method is perhaps most closely related to a recent technique of [8], which is based on the work in [9]. The methods in [9] are used to obtain point-wise mapping by computing descriptors as linear operators, then reducing the number of basis to formulate an approximate linear space, finally recovering the shape correspondence by solving a least squares system. Although it made great progress in mapping points, it has obvious drawbacks: the number of constraints used is too large which limits the use in actual applications. As a result, a novel method is proposed in [8] which extracts more information from the descriptor via commutativity and gets a more accurate result with less linear operators.

Given a pair of models, we want to get correspondence $T$ between source model $M$ and target model $N$. To recover the correspondence $T$, a pipeline which consists of 4 basic steps is described as follows:

- Step 1: Compute the first k eigenfunctions of the Laplace-Beltrami operator. Store them in matrices: $\Phi_M$, $\Phi_N$.
- Step 2: Compute descriptor functions(we use the Scale-invariant heat kernel signatures [2] as the shape descriptor which is robust to scale transformation) on $M$, $N$.Express them in $\Phi_M$, $\Phi_N$, as column of : $A$, $B$.
- Step 3: Solve the following equation:

$$C_{opt} = \arg\min_{C} \parallel CF - G \parallel^2 + \alpha \parallel \Delta_N C - C\Delta_M \parallel^2 \tag{3}$$

where $\Delta_N$, $\Delta_M$ are diagonal matrices of eigenvalues of the Laplace-Beltrami operator and $\alpha$ is a scalar weight.
- Step 4: Convert the functional map $C_{opt}$ to a point to point map $T$.

## 1.3   Measurement of Models

In this paper, we use the measuring method based on geodesic distances to calculate sizes of human body models. In the first place, the 3D point cloud information of the target human body model and the triangular grid information of each vertex is obtained to digitize the 3D human body model. Second, the predicted position of the key feature point is used as the starting point to measure the target human body size. The starting point is regarded as the root node, and the three-dimensional coordinate value of the root node is approximate, and the neighboring points of the root node are bounded by the constraint value, dividing the set of neighboring points of the vertex into left and right subtrees.

Traverse the left and right binary trees of the root node in turn, and find the next closest neighboring point with the root node. The next closest neighboring point becomes the new root node point. According to the points in the edge-tree based on the new root node set. The set of neighboring points is divided into left and right subtrees, and the new root node traverses its left and right binary trees in the same direction. Backtracking until iterate through a leaf node becomes the starting root node and the iterate ended, then the leaf node is the key feature point of the beginning.

Therefore, the shortest path of the contour curve passing through a feature point of the target mannequin can be obtained, and the contour curve passing through the key feature point can be drawn automatically on the target mannequin. Finally, the geodesic distance between two points on the curve is calculated to obtain the geodesic distance of the complete curve passing through the feature point, and obtain the dimension length of the contour curve. Then, the relevant dimension of the 3D human model is normalized to obtain the actual dimension of the corresponding 3D human body.

## 2   Experiment

### 2.1   Parameter Setting of Random Forest Regression

There are six models as the training set and the others as the testing set. Figure 2 shows the relationship between mean square error and computation time cost with different numbers of training models, different sampling rate on each model, different numbers of trees and different sizes of nodes in the regression model. It is known that the slopes represent the value of $\lambda$ from Eq. (2). We observe that the number of trees and models have higher slopes than the size of nodes and the sampling rate. It means that the value of $\lambda_{tr}$ and $\lambda_{sn}$ should be higher than the others. And the value of $\lambda_{no}$ is always the smallest. In other words, the size of nodes has the minimal impact on result while the number of trees and models have more obvious impact. As a result, we increase the number of trees or models while decrease the size of nodes. We set the value of $E_{tree\_n}$ as 40 and the sizes of nodes as 15 to all models while keeping the other $E_X$ fixed. Figure 3 shows compare with [14] in computation time cost and mean square error. The computation time cost of training set and testing set dropped by 10.3% and 10.8%, respectively. The mean error of training set and testing dropped by 9.4% and 17.2%, respectively. It verifies the effectiveness of the proposed method.

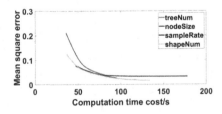

**Fig. 2.** The accuracy and time cost of the regression model

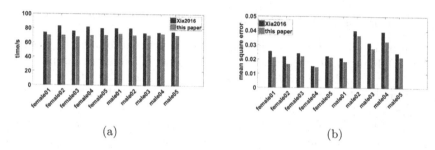

**Fig. 3.** Compare with [14] in computation time cost (a) and mean square error (b)

## 2.2  Correspondence Map

The mapping stage is composed of two parts: mapping of motion sequence, invariant to scale-varying model. The mean Euclidean distance is used to measure the mapping error. The mapping result still has a big error, so we use the Iterative Closest Point(ICP) method to improve the accuracy. The detailed value of it is shown in Table 1. It shows that the accuracy of mapping is more precise with the ICP method and the accuracy improved by about 1.5 times. We use the scale-invariant heat kernel signatures as mentioned in Sect. 1.2 which is robust to scaling transformations. We set four different scales: 0.5 times, 2/3 times, 1.5 times and 2 times. Figure 4 shows the mapping result with different scales. We can see the method is robust to scale transformations and larger scale of scaling brings higher error rate.

**Table 1.** Average mapping error

| Motion | $N_k$ | Mean error | | Motion | $N_k$ | Mean error | |
|---|---|---|---|---|---|---|---|
| | | Before ICP | After ICP | | | Before ICP | After ICP |
| Jumping | 5 | 0.015 | 0.009 | Hanging | 5 | 0.014 | 0.010 |
| | 10 | 0.026 | 0.020 | | 10 | 0.023 | 0.017 |
| | 15 | 0.027 | 0.022 | | 15 | 0.025 | 0.019 |
| Dancing | 5 | 0.014 | 0.009 | Running | 5 | 0.018 | 0.012 |
| | 10 | 0.013 | 0.008 | | 10 | 0.020 | 0.014 |
| | 15 | 0.014 | 0.010 | | 15 | 0.017 | 0.012 |

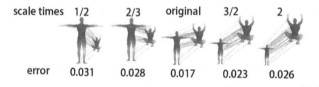

**Fig. 4.** The results of different scale

## 2.3  Measurement of 3D Human Models

We measure the sizes of human body models with different movements as shown in Fig. 5(a). Figure 5(b) illustrates the size changes of different parts of models. It can be seen that different movements bring different size changes. For example, during jumping, the hip circumference mainly changed, while the chest circumference and waist circumference hardly changed. During standing and walking, the sizes of human body change little, that is, the size of the clothes is not required for such movements. In this way, we can estimate whether a particular piece of clothing is suitable for action with the fabric and sizes of the clothes given by the online shop.

Figure 6(a) shows the compare of measurement accuracy with single-source shortest path method proposed in [13]. We can see that the accurate measurement of single-source shortest path is lower than the measurement method proposed in this paper. The accuracy of waist circumference, hip circumference and chest circumference improve 1.1%, 9.2% and 8.3%, respectively. Figure 6(b) shows the compare of mean relative error with method in [13]. It shows that the method proposed in this paper has a lower error, which means that the measurement method in this paper is relatively accurate.

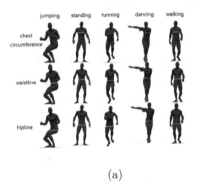
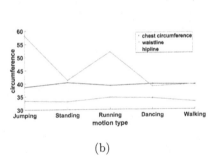

(a)                                        (b)

**Fig. 5.** (a) Different circumference in different motions. (b) Variations in the models' body dimensions

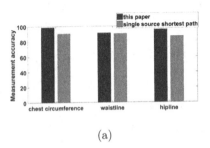
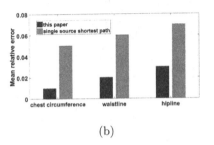

(a)                                        (b)

**Fig. 6.** (a) Measurement accuracy compared with method in [13]. (b) Compare of the mean relative error with method in [13]

## 3    Conclusion

We consider the problem of unsuitable clothing when customers shop online. We use a regression model to get the location of semantic feature points and map the points to motion models. With the feature points on motion models, we can get the sizes of motion models which can help customers buy suitable clothes online. Noisy and partial loss is inevitable for the depth data captured by the 3D scanner. Our work presented in this paper has been optimized for this problem. As shown in Fig. 7, the 3D models have partial loss of arm or leg, the mapping results are still correct.

However, our framework still has some limitations. In the mapping stage, the method computes whole correspondence between source and target model, however, the feature points are defined in some of them. It brings unnecessary time costs. In future work, we will consider local mapping methods instead of point wise mapping.

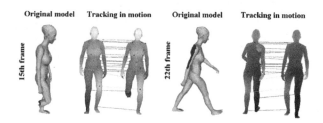

**Fig. 7.** Tracking result with un-complete body models.

## References

1. Blackman, S.: Rigging with mixamo (2014)
2. Bronstein, M.M., Kokkinos, I.: Scale-invariant heat kernel signatures for non-rigid shape recognition. In: Computer Vision & Pattern Recognition (2010)
3. Cordier, F., Lee, W., Seo, H., Magnenat-Thalmann, N.: Virtual-try-on on the web. Laval Virtual (2001)
4. Durupinar, F., Gudukbay, U.: A virtual garment design and simulation system. In: 11th International Conference Information Visualization, IV 2007 (2007)
5. Gültepe, U., Güdükbay, U.: Real-time virtual fitting with body measurement and motion smoothing. Comput. Graphics **43**, 31–43 (2014)
6. ISO, I.: 8559: garment construction and anthropometric surveys-body dimensions. ISO: Switzerland (1989)
7. Izadi, S., Kim, D., Hilliges, O., Molyneaux, D., Fitzgibbon, A.W.: Kinectfusion: real-time 3D reconstruction and interaction using a moving depth camera. In: Proceedings of the 24th Annual ACM Symposium on User Interface Software and Technology, Santa Barbara, CA, USA, 16–19 October 2011 (2011)
8. Nogneng, D., Ovsjanikov, M.: Informative descriptor preservation via commutativity for shape matching. In: Computer Graphics Forum (2017)

9. Ovsjanikov, M., Ben-Chen, M., Solomon, J., Butscher, A., Guibas, L.: Functional maps: a flexible representation of maps between shapes. ACM Trans. Graphics **31**(4), 30 (2012)

10. Pons-Moll, G., Pujades, S., Hu, S., Black, M.J.: Clothcap: seamless 4D clothing capture and retargeting. ACM Trans. Graphics **36**(4CD), 73.1–73.15 (2017)

11. Sitnik, R., Nowak, M., Liberadzki, P., Michoński, J.: 4D scanning system for measurement of human body in motion. Electr. Imaging **2019**(16), 1–2 (2019)

12. Song, D., Li, T., Mao, Z., Liu, A.A.: Sp-viton: shape-preserving image-based virtual try-on network. Multimedia Tools and Applications, pp. 1–13 (2019)

13. jiang tao, Z.: Three-dimensional reconstruction and dimensional measurement of human body based on kinect. Ph.D. thesis (2015)

14. Xia, Q., Shuai, L., Hong, Q., Hao, A.: Automatic extraction of generic focal features on 3d shapes via random forest regression analysis of geodesics-in-heat. Comput. Aided Geometric Des. **49** (2016)

# Amur Tiger Re-ID Based on Locally Guided Adaptive Feature Fusion

Huiling Yu, Changchun Shen, and Yizhuo Zhang[(⊠)]

School of Information and Computer Engineering, Northeast Forestry University,
Harbin, China
yhl@nefu.edu.cn, syx@nefu.edu.cn, nefuzyz@163.com

**Abstract.** Wildlife conservation is crucial to maintaining the stability of ecosystems. Monitoring the population and movement trajectories of endangered species by re-identification (re-ID) is a very promising way for wildlife conservation. The Amur tiger is an endangered species, but there are few studies on Amur tiger re-identification, and the existing methods have deficiencies such as cumbersome processing and low accuracy. In this paper, We introduce a novel locally guided adaptive feature fusion network for the Amur tiger re-ID task, which may help biologists monitor and protect Amur tigers in the wild. The network consists of two parts, global stream and local stream. Especially, The local stream is only used in the training phase, which can not only play the role of pose alignment but also guide and adjust the learning of the Global Stream. In the prediction phase, only global stream is needed, which greatly simplifies the intermediate process compared with the traditional re-ID methods. The experimental results show that our method has achieved high accuracy and efficiency in Amur tiger re-ID task, its performance overtakes the baseline method by a large margin.

**Keywords:** Re-identification · Deep learning · Adaptive feature fusion

## 1 Introduction

With the gradual deterioration of ecological environment and the gradual loss of species diversity, the stability of the ecosystem is facing severe challenges. How to apply computer vision technology to the protection and monitoring of wildlife has become a highly concerned issue. The Amur Tiger is one of the largest living cats in the world, mainly distributed in Siberia of Russia, North Korea and northeast China. In recent years, due to human poaching and habitat destruction, the population of Amur tigers has declined sharply, and they are classified as an endangered species. Therefore, if the re-ID technology can be used to identify and monitor the Amur tiger, their movement trajectory, range of activities, and living habits can be effectively analyzed. This work will help biologists take further measures to protect and save wild Amur tigers.

The previous animal re-ID technology has not been well developed, on the one hand, the relevant datasets have defects such as small scale, limited annotations,

© Springer Nature Switzerland AG 2020
F. Tian et al. (Eds.): CASA 2020, CCIS 1300, pp. 101–111, 2020.
https://doi.org/10.1007/978-3-030-63426-1_11

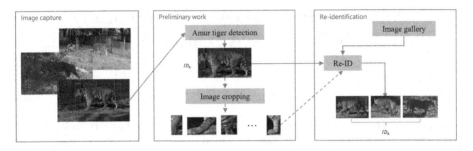

**Fig. 1.** Flow chart of Amur tiger re-ID system. It consists of three modules: (1) Image capture. It is mainly responsible for collecting images of Amur tigers in the wild. (2) Preliminary work. This module is mainly used for Amur tiger detection and image cropping, the latter will only be used during the training phase. (3) Re-identification. The results of the previous module and the re-ID algorithm are used for Amur tiger re-ID. Note that the steps shown by the dotted lines in the figure only appear during the training phase.

and capturing under unnatural conditions. On the other hand, the differences in appearance between animals of the same species are not as obvious as human. To this end, Li et al. [5] introduced the ATRW dataset for the study of Amur tiger re-ID, and proposed a special method, which includes Amur tiger detection, pose estimation, and re-identification. However, The method is not only complex but also unsatisfactory.

To address the above problems, we introduce a novel locally guided adaptive feature fusion network (LAFFNet) for Amur tiger re-ID task. The network mainly includes two parts, global stream and local stream. In the global stream, we extract feature vectors from the same pictures with three different size ratios, and then form the final global feature through adaptive fusion. The local stream is used to extract local features from the cropped body parts images, and plays the role of pose alignment, guiding and adjusting the learning of the global stream. In the prediction phase, only global stream is required. Experimental results show that our method achieves high accuracy and efficiency, and its performance far exceeds the baseline method. In summary, the contributions of our work are:

- We constructed a framework for Amur tiger re-ID system as shown in Fig. 1.
- We introduced a novel locally guided adaptive feature fusion network for Amur tiger re-ID task, which mainly consists of two parts, global stream and local stream. The local stream is used to guide and adjust the learning of the global stream. In the prediction phase, only global stream is required, which greatly simplifies the Amur tiger re-ID process.
- The trained model was tested on ATRW dataset and compared with the baseline method. Experimental results show that the method proposed in this paper is superior to the baseline method in both mAP and top-k accuracy by a large margin.

## 2   Related Work

In the early days, the term re-identification (re-ID) was not proposed, but such tasks are often closely related to multi-camera tracking. As early as 1997, Huang and Russell [4] proposed to use Bayesian formula to evaluate the posterior probability of appearance characteristics of objects in a surveillance video under other devices. In 2005, researchers at the University of Amsterdam first proposed the concept of "Person Re-Identification" [12], and defined person re-ID as "recognizing a person who left the field of vision and re-entered the field of vision". Since then, many datasets on person re-ID have been published, and many scholars have begun to conduct research on re-ID. Since 2014, deep learning has been applied to the field of re-ID, which makes full use of large-scale datasets, coupled with the performance improvement of computer hardware, makes the field of re-ID burst unprecedented vitality.

For a long time, the main targets of re-ID were person and vehicles, since these objects are closely related to our daily life and have easily distinguishable appearances. Re-ID can play a vital role in intelligent security, trajectory tracking, video surveillance and many other fields. In recent years, several large-scale person re-ID datasets have been introduced, such as Market-1501, DukeMTMC-reID, and CUHK03. This provides support for research on person re-ID and improvement of related algorithms. In addition, there are some re-ID datasets about animals, such as elephants, whales and tigers. However, these datasets have various shortcomings, such as small amount of data, low image resolution, and limited annotations. These defects also slow the development of animal re-ID. In response to these problems, Li et al. [5] introduced the ATRW dataset. This dataset is larger than the previous animal re-ID dataset, with detailed bounding boxes, pose keypoints, and identity annotations, and was captured in natural conditions. However, there are still many challenges in Amur tiger re-ID, such as different degrees of occlusion, poor lighting conditions, low image resolution, and unrestricted background environment as shown in Fig. 2.

With the development of re-ID technology and more and more datasets being proposed, researchers began to notice the great potential of re-ID in wildlife conservation, and gradually expanded the scope of re-ID research from person and vehicles to wildlife. In 2005, Arzoumanian et al. [2] used an astronomical algorithm to identify star patterns to analyze the unique spot pattern on the side of the whale shark to explore the method of re-ID of the whale shark. In 2007, Ardovini et al. [1] introduced multi-curve matching to re-identify elephants from images. In 2014, Carter et al. [3] adopted an integrated method of training multiple different networks to re-identify green turtles based on turtle shell patterns. This method is currently used to monitor green turtle populations. In 2017, Weideman et al. [10] introduced a novel method that combines integral curvature representation and two matching algorithms to identify cetaceans through their fins. In 2019, while introducing the ATRW dataset, Li et al. [5] proposed a novel Amur tiger re-ID method, which introduced precise pose parts modeling in deep neural networks to deal with tiger's large pose variation. However, this method is not suitable for direct application to the re-ID of wild Amur tigers.

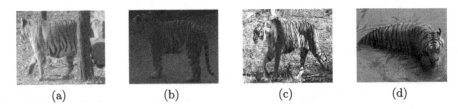

(a)                 (b)                 (c)                 (d)

**Fig. 2.** Example images of ATRW dataset. There are many challenges in Amur tiger re-ID task, for example: (a) Different degrees of occlusion. (b) Poor lighting conditions. (c) Low image resolution. (d) Unrestricted background environment.

First, the processing of this method is more complicated, mainly including Amur tiger detection, pose estimation, and re-identification. In addition, the effect of this method is actually not ideal. Its efficiency and accuracy have not yet reached the standard for application in the wild. This also shows that there is still much room for improvement in the field of animal re-ID. Later, Liu et al. [6] proposed a novel PPGNet for Amur tiger re-ID. The PPGNet contains three branches with one full stream and two part streams. The part streams are used to guide the full stream in learning and aligning the local features. It can achieve excellent performance in the inference stage even without the part streams. However, the structure of PPGNet is complicated, with too many branches and parameters, which may affect the training speed and effect. In addition, they did not take into account the width and aspect ratios distribution of the bounding boxes in the dataset. Our method was inspired by PPGNet by Liu et al. [6], and made many improvements on this basis.

## 3    Methodology

### 3.1    Partial Image

In some person re-ID methods, algorithms such as pose estimation are used for image alignment and normalization, or accurate pose modeling [9,14]. In this study, this kind of thinking was not adopted, since it is cumbersome and requires complete keypoint annotations. For general datasets, they have limited annotations and there is occlusion in many images. These factors will have a negative impact on pose estimation, and may further affect the accuracy of Amur tiger re-ID. In this study, we adopt the method of Liu et al. [6] to crop the image of the Amur tiger into 7 parts according to the keypoints. Then these cropped part images are fed into the local stream of the network. On the one hand, the step of pose estimation is omitted. On the other hand, it is helpful for the alignment and normalization of the image. Due to part of the Amur tiger in some images is occluded or lack of keypoint annotations, not every image of the Amur tiger can get all part images.

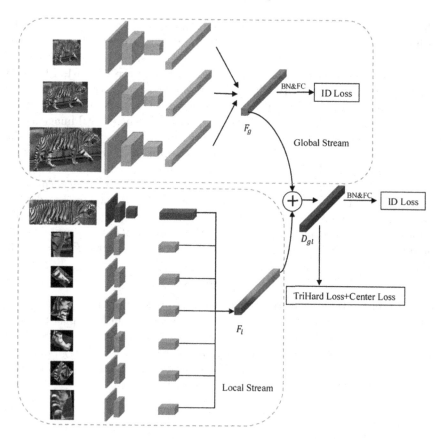

**Fig. 3.** The structure of our proposed network (LAFFNet). It consists of two parts: global stream and local stream. The global stream is the main stream, which is used to extract the global feature from the full Amur tiger images, and the local stream is the auxiliary stream, which is used to extract the local feature from the cropped part images. The Local Stream is only used during the training phase.

## 3.2 Locally Guided Adaptive Feature Fusion Network

Figure 3 shows the LAFFNet structure. The network is mainly composed of global stream and local stream. Inspired by the PPGNet of Liu et al. [6] and the DAS-reID of Zhang et al. [13], we take the global stream as the main stream, extract the global features from the full Amur tiger image, then perform adaptive feature fusion, and extract local features from part images of Amur tigers. Finally, the global stream is sufficient for the purpose of Amur tiger re-identification.

**Global Stream.** In the global stream, the input is the full image of the Amur tiger, as shown in the upper left of Fig. 3. Inspired by the Adaptively Spatial Feature Fusion proposed by Liu et al. [7], we constructed a three-branch network in the global stream for feature extraction of the full images of the Amur tiger. The inputs of the three branches come from the same image, but their sizes and aspect ratios are different. Specifically, we first scale the input image to different sizes and aspect ratios, where the input sizes are $64 \times 64$, $128 \times 216$ and $256 \times 512$ (*height* $\times$ *width*). Their corresponding aspect ratios are 1:1, 1.69:1 and 2:1, respectively. The reason for this is based on statistical analysis of the dataset. According to the statistical result, we choose some typical image aspect ratios as the input image aspect ratios, since they cover most of the image size distribution. Then, these scaled images are input into the three-branch network for feature extraction. Here, the ResNet101, which was pretrained on ImageNet dataset, was selected as the backbone of the network. After that, each of the three branches extracts a 2048-dimension vector $F_g^i$ $(i = 1, 2, 3)$. In the adaptive feature fusion stage, instead of directly adding the elements at the corresponding positions or concatenating along channels, the global features $F_g$ are obtained by adaptively adding the three previously obtained feature vector $F_g^i$ $(i = 1, 2, 3)$ as in (1).

$$y_{ij} = \alpha_{ij} x_{ij}^1 + \beta_{ij} x_{ij}^2 + \gamma_{ij} x_{ij}^3 \tag{1}$$

where $y_{ij}$ represents the feature value at the $(i, j)$ position of the global feature $F_g$. $x_{ij}^l, l = 1, 2, 3$, respectively represent the feature values at $(i, j)$ positions corresponding to the three branches of the feature pyramid. $\alpha_{ij}, \beta_{ij}, \gamma_{ij}$ respectively represent the weight coefficients corresponding to the position of $(i, j)$, and they are learned from the network training. The value range of them is $[0, 1]$, and the sum of the coefficients at the corresponding position is 1:

$$\alpha_{ij} + \beta_{ij} + \gamma_{ij} = 1 \tag{2}$$

**Local Stream.** In the local stream, we take part images cropped from the full Amur tiger images as the input images. According to the keypoints of the Amur tiger given in the ATRW dataset, we crop out seven part images from each full image, namely the body, left and right front legs, left and right hind thighs, and left and right hind shanks. Then separately input these part images into a network for feature extraction. Since the cropped part images contain less feature details, the ResNet34 residual network is used as the backbone. Due to the distinguishable features of tigers are mainly the body stripes, we purposely increased the size of the Amur tiger's body image, and used the complete ResNet34 network to perform feature extraction on the body image of the Amur tiger. After adaptive average pooling, we obtained a 512-dimensional body feature map $F_l^1$. For the feature extraction of the other six part images, only the first three parts of ResNet34 are used. After adaptive average pooling, a total of six 256-dimensional limb features map $F_l^i, i = 2, 3..., 7$ are obtained. Finally, the seven part feature vectors $F_l^i, i = 1, 2..., 7$ are concatenated along channels to form a complete local feature $F_l$ with the same dimension as the global feature $F_g$.

### 3.3   Feature Fusion

In order to make use of the body stripes and body features of the Amur tiger, so as to guide the global stream to better learn from the full image and facilitate the alignment of the body parts of the Amur tiger, we add the corresponding elements of the global feature $F_g$ and the local feature $F_l$.

$$D_{gl} = F_g + F_l \tag{3}$$

where $D_{gl}$ represents the fused feature of global feature $F_g$ and local feature $F_l$.

The fused feature $D_{gl}$ is jointly determined by the global feature $F_g$ and the local feature $F_l$. In the training phase, when performing backpropagation, the global stream will be affected by the local stream and the network parameters will be updated.

### 3.4   Loss Function

For re-ID task, the triplet loss is often used. Here, we use TriHard loss to optimize our network. The specific loss function is defined as:

$$L_{TriH} = \frac{1}{P \times K} \sum_{a \in batch} \left( \max_{p \in A} d_{a,p} - \min_{n \in B} d_{a,n} + \alpha \right)_+ \tag{4}$$

where $(z)_+$ means $\max(z, 0)$, $P$ and $K$ represent a batch contains $P$ IDs and each ID corresponds to $K$ images. For each image in a batch, $A$ represents the corresponding positive sample set and $B$ represents the corresponding negative sample set, choose the positive sample that is farthest away to form a positive sample pair, ie $\max_{p \in A} d_{a,p}$, and choose the nearest negative sample to form a negative sample pair, ie $\min_{n \in B} d_{a,n}$. $\alpha$ is a manually set threshold value, which is 0.3 here. The Euclidean Distance calculation formula is used here.

In this paper, the LAFFNet is optimized by the combination of Cross Entropy Loss (ID Loss) and TriHard Loss. These two kinds of loss functions are also the most commonly used in the field of re-ID. Firstly, the global feature $F_g$ and the local feature $F_l$ are fused to obtain the feature $D_{gl}$, which increases the information of the feature. Then the fused feature $D_{gl}$ is used to calculate the triplet loss and center loss. The fused feature $D_{gl}$ is followed by a batch normalization layer and a fully connected layer, and then the cross-entropy loss is calculated.

Since Triplet Loss only considers the relative distance between samples, which means it only cares about the inter-class gap, not whether the intra-class is compact. In order to improve the clustering performance of the network, we introduce Center Loss [11]. The formula is defined as:

$$L_c = \frac{1}{2} \sum_{i=1}^{B} \| f_i - c_{y_i} \|_2^2 \tag{5}$$

where $B$ is the number of samples in a mini-batch, $f_i$ is the feature representation of the $i$-th sample, $y_i$ is the label of the $i$-th sample in a mini-batch, and $c_{y_i}$ is the center of the class to which the sample belongs.

For the cross-entropy loss in the global stream, the global feature $F_g$ is also followed by a batch normalization layer and a fully connected layer. In the final prediction phase, the result of the global stream is used as the final judgment basis, and no local stream is needed.

Finally, we use a combined loss function to train the entire network, which is defined as

$$L = L_{TriH} + L_{ID_g} + L_{ID_{gl}} + L_c \qquad (6)$$

where $L_{TriH}$ represents the TriHard loss, $L_{ID_g}$ represents the cross-entropy loss of the global stream, $L_{ID_{gl}}$ represents the cross-entropy loss calculated using the fusion feature $D_{gl}$, $L_c$ represents the center loss.

## 4    Experiment

### 4.1    Dataset

The ATRW dataset proposed by Li et al. [5] is used in the experiment, which includs 8076 video clips of Amur tigers, all of which were collected from 92 amur tigers. This dataset is larger, more detailed and captured in natural conditions than the general animal rei-ID dataset. Since the stripes on both sides of the body of the Amur tiger are different, images collected from different sides of the same Amur tiger are usually marked with different IDs, so there are altogether 182 entities in the dataset, that is, there are 182 IDs. During the training phase, only 1887 images were actually available, since they provide explicit IDs and keypoints. In the test set, there are 1764 images.

### 4.2    Experiment Details

**Data Augmentation.** In order to increase the amount of data in the training set and improve the generalization capability of the model, we mainly applied data augmentation methods such as horizontal flipping, random cropping and random erasing to the images in the training set in the experiment. In addition, some other measures were taken, such as randomly changing their brightness, contrast and saturation within the range of 0.8–1.2, and randomly rotating them within the range of $-10$–$10\,°$.

**Training Tricks.** We adopted the Warmup strategy to adjust the learning rate of our network. The Warmup strategy can help alleviate the overfitting of the model at the initial stage and help maintain the stability of the deep network. Besides, we also adopted other tircks such as label smoothing, BNNeck [8], and center loss to optimize our network, which not only improved our model's constraint capability and clustering performance but also accelerated the model's convergence.

Table 1. Comparison of our method with the baseline.

| Setting | Method | | Single-Cam | | | Cross-Cam | | |
|---------|--------|---|------|-------|-------|------|-------|-------|
|         |        |   | mAP  | top-1 | top-5 | mAP  | top-1 | top-5 |
| Plain | Baseline [5] | CE | 59.1 | 78.6 | 92.7 | 38.1 | 69.7 | 87.8 |
|       |              | Triplet loss | 71.3 | 86.6 | 96.0 | 47.2 | 77.6 | 90.6 |
|       |              | Aligned-reID | 64.8 | 81.2 | 92.4 | 44.2 | 73.8 | 90.5 |
|       |              | PPbM-a | 74.1 | 88.2 | 96.4 | 51.7 | 76.8 | 91.0 |
|       |              | PPbM-b | 72.8 | 89.4 | 95.6 | 47.8 | 77.1 | 90.7 |
|       | **our method(LAFFNet)** | | **88.9** | **98.3** | **98.6** | **60.7** | **92.0** | **97.7** |
| Wild | Baseline [5] | CE | 58.8 | 78.7 | 92.5 | 34.5 | 68.5 | 86.8 |
|      |              | Triplet loss | 70.7 | 86.5 | 95.1 | 45.2 | 77.6 | 90.5 |
|      |              | Aligned-reID | 58.7 | 74.8 | 90.7 | 41.0 | 70.1 | 87.2 |
|      |              | PPbM-a | 71.0 | 87.4 | 96.6 | 50.3 | 77.2 | 90.7 |
|      |              | PPbM-b | 69.2 | 88.9 | 95.3 | 46.2 | 76.6 | 91.2 |
|      | **our method(LAFFNet)** | | **83.8** | **93.3** | 96.4 | **55.7** | **88.8** | **93.1** |

### 4.3 Experimental Results

The test of Amur tiger re-ID in this experiment is divided into two cases, plain tiger re-ID and wild tiger re-ID. According to the different collection situations of images, we divide them into single-camera set and cross-camera set. The single-camera means that the images of one Amur tiger were only taken by a single camera, and the cross-camera means that the images of one Amur tiger were taken by more than one camera. As with the general re-ID method, we use mean average precision (mAP) and top-k ($k = 1, 5$) accuracy to evaluate our method. Here are the results of our experiment.

**Plain Tiger Re-ID.** In the plain tiger re-ID, we adopt the plain Amur tiger re-ID test set, and the data are all single Amur tiger images cropped according to the bounding boxes, with precise identification and keypoint annotations. Table 1 shows the comparison between our method and the baseline method. In the plain setting, it can be seen that our method achieves the highest accuracy among the six evaluation indicators and overtakes the baseline method by a large margin. In particular, the mAP in single-cam case is improved by 14.8% compared to the baseline method, and the top-1 accuracy in cross-cam case is improved by 14.4%.

**Wild Tiger Re-ID.** In the wild tiger re-ID, we adopt the wild Amur tiger re-ID test set, which contains unprocessed original images of the Amur tiger without any annotations. First, we need a special detector to detect Amur tiger individuals from the original image. We adopt the modified and retrained YOLOv3

**Table 2.** Comparison of Plain tiger re-ID and Wild tiger re-ID.

| Setting | mmAP | Single-Cam | | | Cross-Cam | | |
|---------|------|------|-------|-------|------|-------|-------|
| | | mAP | top-1 | top-5 | mAP | top-1 | top-5 |
| Plain | 74.8 | 88.9 | 98.3 | 98.6 | 60.7 | 92.0 | 97.7 |
| Wild | 69.7 | 83.8 | 93.3 | 96.4 | 55.7 | 88.8 | 93.1 |

as the detector to perform Amur tiger detection on the original images since it is open-sourced and shows great performance in Amur tiger detection. Table 1 shows the comparison between our method and the baseline method. In the wild setting, our method also improves a lot compared to the baseline method in performance, especially, the mAP in single-cam case and the top-1 accuracy in cross-cam case are improved by 12.8% and 11.2%, respectively.

**Comparison of the Two Cases.** The test results of our method in plain and wild settings are shown in Table 2. Among them, mmAP represents the average of mAP on both single-cam case and cross-cam case, which reflects the comprehensive level of our method. Obviously, the performance of our method is better in the plain setting than in the wild setting. The mmAP of plain test result is about 5% higher than that of wild test result. In fact, this result is expected. In plain Amur tiger re-ID test, the test data are all processed and with clear annotations, while in wild Amur tiger re-ID test, the test data are all original images. In fact, it is also the dataset of Amur tiger detection. When capturing the original images, there are different degrees of occlusion, unrestricted lighting conditions and complex natural backgrounds in the wild environment. Therefore, data preprocessing including Amur tiger detection must be performed before the wild dataset can be utilized. A better tiger detector can help us better detect and crop single Amur tiger images from the original images, which is more conducive to Amur tiger re-ID.

## 5    Conclusion

In this paper, we propose a novel locally guided adaptive feature fusion network (LAFFNet) for the Amur tiger re-ID task. In this network, we introduced an adaptive multi-scale feature fusion method in global stream to extract more robust global features from the full images of the Amur tiger. The local stream is used to extract local features from cropped part images, and it also plays the role of pose alignment and guiding the learning of global stream. In particular, the local stream is only used in the training phase. We only need to input a full Amur tiger image into the global stream to get the Amur tiger re-ID result, which greatly simplifies the intermediate process compared with the traditional re-ID method. Compared with the baseline method, our method has significant improvement in accuracy and efficiency. Nevertheless, we believe that there is still much room for improvement in Amur tiger re-ID, and we will continue to work on computer vision and wildlife conservation in the future.

**Acknowledgments.** We would like to thank WWF and MakerCollider for their efforts to collect raw dataset. Thanks to CVWC for making the ATRW dataset and promoting the research of Amur tiger re-identification. This work is supported by the Fundamental Research Funds for the Central Universities (No. 2572017CB34).

# References

1. Ardovini, A., Cinque, L., Sangineto, E.: Identifying elephant photos by multi-curve matching. Pattern Recogn. **41**(6), 1867–1877 (2008)
2. Arzoumanian, Z., Holmberg, J., Norman, B.: An astronomical pattern-matching algorithm for computer-aided identification of whale sharks Rhincodon Typus. J. Appl. Ecol. **42**(6), 999–1011 (2005)
3. Carter, S.J.B., Bell, I., Miller, J., Gash, P.P.: Automated marine turtle photograph identification using artificial neural networks, with application to green turtles. J. Exp. Mar. Biol. Ecol. **452**, 105–110 (2014)
4. Huang, T., Russell, S.: Object identification in a Bayesian context, pp. 1276–1282 (1997)
5. Li, S., Li, J., Lin, W., Tang, H.: Amur tiger re-identification in the wild. In: arXiv: Computer Vision and Pattern Recognition (2019)
6. Liu, C., Zhang, R., Guo, L.: Part-pose guided amur tiger re-identification (2019)
7. Liu, S., Huang, D., Wang, Y.: Learning spatial fusion for single-shot object detection. In: arXiv: Computer Vision and Pattern Recognition (2019)
8. Luo, H., Gu, Y., Liao, X., Lai, S., Jiang, W.: Bag of tricks and a strong baseline for deep person re-identification (2019)
9. Suruliandi, A., Poongothai, E.: Person re-identification based on pose angle estimation and multi-feature extraction. IET Biometrics **7**(4), 365–370 (2018)
10. Weideman, H.J., Jablons, et al.: Integral curvature representation and matching algorithms for identification of dolphins and whales, pp. 2831–2839 (2017)
11. Wen, Y., Zhang, K., Li, Z., Qiao, Y.: A discriminative feature learning approach for deep face recognition, pp. 499–515 (2016)
12. Zajdel, W., Zivkovic, Z., Krose, B.J.A.: Keeping track of humans: have i seen this person before?, pp. 2081–2086 (2005)
13. Zhang, Z., Lan, C., Zeng, W., Chen, Z.: Densely semantically aligned person re-identification, pp. 667–676 (2019)
14. Zheng, L., Huang, Y., Lu, H., Yang, Y.: Pose invariant embedding for deep person re-identification. arXiv: Computer Vision and Pattern Recognition (2017)

# MVFNN: Multi-Vision Fusion Neural Network for Fake News Picture Detection

Junxiao Xue[1], Yabo Wang[1(✉)], Shuning Xu[1], Lei Shi[1(✉)], Lin Wei[1], and Huawei Song[2]

[1] School of Software, Zhengzhou University, Zhengzhou 450002, China
`wangyb@stu.zzu.edu.cn`, `shilei@zzu.edu.cn`
[2] Zhongyuan Network Security Research Institute, Zhengzhou 450002, China

**Abstract.** During this year's Novel Coronavirus (2019-nCoV) outbreak, the spread of fake news has caused serious social panic. This fact necessitates a focus on fake news detection. Pictures could be viewed as fake news indicators and hence could be used to identify fake news effectively. However, fake news pictures detection is more challenging since fake news picture identification is more difficult than the fake picture recognition. This paper proposes a multi-vision fusion neural network (MVFNN) which consists of four main components: the visual modal module, the visual feature fusion module, the physical feature module and the ensemble module. The visual modal module is responsible for extracting image features from images pixel domain, frequency domain, and tamper detection. It cooperates with the visual features fusion module to detect fake news images from multi-vision fusion. And the ensemble module combines visual features and physical features to detect the fake news pictures. Experimental results show that our model could achieve better detection performance by at least 4.29% than the existing methods in benchmark datasets.

**Keywords:** Fake news pictures · Deep learning · Multi-vision domain

## 1 Introduction

The rise of social platforms such as Weibo and Twitter not only brings convenience to users, but also provides soil for the breeding and dissemination of fake news. The frantic spread of fake news has had many negative effects. Take the Novel Coronavirus (2019-nCoV) in 2020 as an example, the spread of various fake news caused serious social panic during the virus outbreak. Fake news seriously harms the harmony and stability of society [1,2], which necessitates the effective automated fake news detection [3–5].

The work was supported by the National Key Research and Development Program of China: No. 2018******400, and the training plan of young backbone teachers in colleges and universities of Henan Province.

© Springer Nature Switzerland AG 2020
F. Tian et al. (Eds.): CASA 2020, CCIS 1300, pp. 112–119, 2020.
https://doi.org/10.1007/978-3-030-63426-1_12

Pictures are always important parts of the news. Studies have shown that the spread range of the news containing pictures is wider than the one without pictures by 11 times [6]. Fake news always use provocative pictures to attract and mislead readers as well. Therefore, an effective way to identify fake news pictures would help to detect the fake news. Actually, one important potential remedy for fake news recognition is to make use of the visual modal content of the news. Jin et al. found that the fake news pictures were statistically different from those of real news  [6]. For example, the number of pictures illustrated in the news, the proportion of news containing hot pictures, and the proportion of special pictures (such as long pictures, chat screenshots, etc.) are also frequently used as statistical features for detection. Compared with fake pictures detection, fake news pictures detection is a more challenging task. This is because fake news pictures are more diverse. As shown in the Fig. 1, fake news pictures mainly have the following types: **1.** The tampered news picture: the picture is maliciously tampered to mislead the readers. **2.** The misleading picture: the picture itself is real but it is misinterpreted with the text description.

(a)                                                    (b)

**Fig. 1.** Some fake news pictures, (a) are tampered news pictures. (b) are misleading pictures that pictures don't match text.

The main contribution of this paper is:

- A new fake news image detection model is proposed, which can effectively identify fake news images by combining image tampering information, semantic information, frequency domain information and statistical characteristics.
- The validity of the proposed model is verified by a large number of experiments on two real datasets.

The organization of the rest paper is as follows: the related works are reviewed in the next section. In Sect. 3, we provide a detailed description of our proposed model. The experimental results and analysis is presented in Sect. 4. Finally, our conclusions are summarized in Sect. 5.

## 2    Related Works

In the fake news detection task, in addition to text content, visual information is an important part of fake news detection. With the spread of multimedia content, researchers have begun to include visual information in the detection of fake news.

Some early methods based on machine learning used basic statistical characteristics [8], such as the number of pictures in the news, the proportion of news with popular pictures. However, these handmade characteristics time-consuming, laborious and limited to study complex patterns, lead to fake news detection task of poor generalization performance.

Visual forensic features are usually used in image processing detection. Some works extract visual forensic features to assess the authority of the attached images [7]. However, these forensic features are mostly hand-made and used to detect specific traces of manipulation, which is not applicable for fake news of real pictures [9].

Since the Convolutional Neural Network (CNN) has been verified to be effective in image classification [10], most existing multimedia content-based works use pre-trained deep CNNs, such as VGG19, to obtain general visual representations and fuse them with text information [10–13]. The first work incorporating multi-modal contents on the social networks via deep neural networks in fake news detection was reported in Ref [12], in which Wang et al. proposed an end-to-end event adversarial neural network to detect newly emerged fake news based on multi-modal features. Khattar et al. [13] proposed a new method to learn multi-modal information sharing representation for fake news detection. But due to the lack of task-related information, the visual features they adopted were too general to reflect the inherent characteristics of fake news pictures.The MVNN model proposed by Qi combined the information of pictures in both physical and semantic levels, however, it did not perform deep feature mining and was dedicated for particular field of fake new pictures [14].

In order to overcome these limitations, a new deep network combining visual modal features and physical features is proposed to detect fake news images.

## 3   The Proposed Model

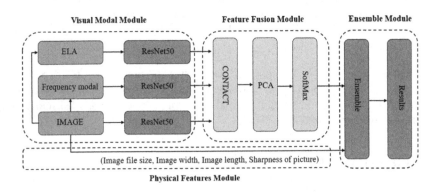

**Fig. 2.** The framework of our proposed MVFNN.

## 3.1 Model Overview

In this work, we designed a method which could conduct image tampering detection, image semantic detection and frequency domain detection simultaneously to explore the different visual patterns of fake news images in various visual modalities and extract effective features. At the same time, it combines the physical features such as the clarity, big or small and size of images to detect the fake news pictures. The model is shown in Fig. 2.

## 3.2 Model Derivation

In this part, we show and derive modules of the model, the details are as follows:

In the tamper detection part, we first apply the error-level analysis (ELA) algorithm on the input images. The main idea of ELA is based on the fact that the tampered region of the image is significantly different from the original one after a fixed-quality compression, and the location of the tampered region is obtained accordingly, as shown in Fig. 3. For the ELA processed images, we used the pre-trained ResNet50 to extract features. In addition, we added a 2048-neuron fully-connected layer to the ResNet50 in order to obtain the feature vectors denoted as $F_t = [v_1^t, v_2^t, v_3^t, \dots, v_{2048}^t]^T$.

In the semantic detection part, we directly use the pre-trained ResNet50 to extract the features of the input images. The extracted features can be expressed as $F_s = [v_1^s, v_2^s, v_3^s, \dots, v_{2048}^s]^T$.

Considering that the image recompression can be well reflected in the frequency domain, we first split it into three channels of RGB, and then conduct Discrete Cosine Transform (DCT) in three channels respectively. After that, they are combined together, and then a Fourier transform is performed on the picture to obtain the feature representation in the frequency domain. The features are subsequently used as the inputs to the ResNet50.

In the physical feature module, we use the size of the image file, the length of the image, the width of the image, and the quantification value of the sharpness of the image as the physical features to detect the fake news image, that is $F_p = [p_1, p_2, p_3, p_4]$. To calculate the quantized value of the image, we first use the $3 \times 3$ Laplace operator to do the convolution operation on the original image, and then take the variance of the convolution operation result as the quantized value of the image.

In the feature fusion module, for the feature $F_t = [v_1^t, v_2^t, v_3^t, \dots, v_{2048}^t]^T, F_s = [v_1^s, v_2^s, v_3^s, \dots, v_{2048}^s]^T$ and $F_f = [v_1^f, v_2^f, v_3^f, \dots, v_{2048}^f]^T$ extracted by ResNet50, we firstly concatenate the features, namely get a new feature vector $F_c = [F_t, F_s, F_f]^T$. Considering the high feature dimension after extraction, we use PCA to reduce the dimension of extracted features by mapping the feature vector of 6144 dimensions to the feature vector of 1024 dimensions in order to obtain more compact features.

In the end, in the ensemble module, we combine the physical features of the image and the visual modal prediction results of the image, that is $F_a = [p, p_1, p_2, p_3, p_4]$, and then use XGBoost to identify the final fake news image.

**Fig. 3.** Images processed by ELA. We can clearly see the tampered part.

## 4    Experiments

### 4.1    Datasets

In this paper we use the dataset (D1) [17] provided by the Zhiyuan Fake News Recognition Competition and the dataset (D2) used in the literature [16]. D1 contains 20459 real news pictures, 13636 fake news pictures, all images are from the news on Weibo. D2 contains 3725 real news pictures, 2804 fake news pictures, which are from the well-known authoritative news websites (such as The New York Times, The Washington Post, etc.)

### 4.2    Baselines

In this section, in order to evaluate the effectiveness of our proposed method, we selected several representative fake news picture detection methods as the baseline.

- **Forensics features (FF)+LR:** Ref [13] employed image forensics features in detecting fake news. Logistic regression algorithm was used as the classifier.
- **Pre-trained VGG19:** Pre-trained VGG is widely used as a feature extractor for detection of multi-modal fake news [13].
- **ConvAE:** Autoencoder (AE) is an artificial neural network learning efficient data representation in an unsupervised manner [15].
- **MVNN:** The MVNN model covers the visual content of the physical and semantic levels of pictures [14].

### 4.3    Performance Comparison

The comparison results between the proposed method and the baseline methods on D1 and D2 are shown in Tabel 1. It can be observed that the proposed MVFNN in this paper could significantly improve the ACC, F1 and AUC as compared with the baseline methods. For the D1 dataset, the accuracy was improved by 26.87%, 19.34%, 18.18%, 4.29% as compared with FF+LR, VGG19 (Pre-trained), ConvAE, MVNN, respectively. This shows that our model can capture the inherent characteristics of fake news pictures effectively.

**Table 1.** Performance comparison between different methods on the D1 and D2.

| Method | D1 | | | D2 | | |
|---|---|---|---|---|---|---|
| | ACC | F1 | AUC | ACC | F1 | AUC |
| FF+LR | 0.6654 | 0.6892 | 0.6603 | 0.6832 | 0.6763 | 0.6831 |
| VGG19(Pre-trained) | 0.7407 | 0.7911 | 0.7324 | 0.7083 | 0.7001 | 0.7034 |
| ConvAE | 0.7523 | 0.7674 | 0.7498 | 0.7328 | 0.7263 | 0.7315 |
| MVNN | 0.8912 | 0.9085 | 0.8902 | 0.8387 | 0.8172 | 0.8327 |
| **MVFNN(Ours)** | **0.9341** | **0.9453** | **0.9338** | **0.8853** | **0.8786** | **0.8832** |

### 4.4 Ablation Study

To visually demonstrate the effectiveness of different network components, we designed some internal model comparisons to simplify the MVFNN variant by removing some components:

- **Tamper:** features of the picture after ELA to detect fake news pictures.
- **Physical Features:** physical features are used to determine the authenticity of the image.
- **Tamper+Semantics:** features of tamper detection and semantic detection are integrated to identify fake news pictures.
- **Tamper+Semantics+Frequency Domain:** the features of the tamper detection are fused with the features of the semantic detection and the features of the frequency domain detection to identify fake news pictures.
- **PCA:** PCA is added to reduce the dimension of the fused feature.

The results of the ablation study are reported in Table 2 and we can find that each of network components is a contribution. Meanwhile, we compared the performance of Random Forests and XGBoost in the integration module,

**Table 2.** Individual performance of each module on D1 and D2.

| Method | D1 | | | D2 | | |
|---|---|---|---|---|---|---|
| | ACC | F1 | AUC | ACC | F1 | AUC |
| Tamper(ResNet50) | 0.8519 | 0.8800 | 0.8523 | 0.7687 | 0.7235 | 0.7638 |
| Physical Features(XGBoost) | 0.8910 | 0.9077 | 0.8858 | 0.8734 | 0.8724 | 0.8716 |
| Tamper+Semantics | 0.8960 | 0.9122 | 0.8913 | 0.8307 | 0.8120 | 0.8307 |
| Tamper+Semantics+ Frequency | 0.9012 | 0.9189 | 0.8998 | 0.8314 | 0.8138 | 0.8324 |
| PCA | 0.9083 | 0.9253 | 0.9023 | 0.8368 | 0.8214 | 0.8354 |
| MVFNN(RF) | 0.9298 | 0.9355 | 0.9301 | 0.8802 | 0.8654 | 0.8792 |
| **MVFNN(XGBoost)** | **0.9341** | **0.9453** | **0.9338** | **0.8853** | **0.8786** | **0.8832** |

and the experiments proved that XGBoost performs better on both datasets, which means that XGBoost is more suitable for fake news image detection.

## 4.5   Multi-feature Fusion

In this section, we evaluated different feature fusion schemes. Since some existing models used attention mechanism to fuse features, we employed PCA, Attention, PCA+Attention, and Attention+PCA to conduct the feature fusion. PCA represents that only PCA is used to reduce the dimension of features in the feature fusion part. Attention represents the use of an attentional mechanism to assign weight to the feature; PCA+Attention represents the one that applies PCA dimensionality reduction followed by the attention layer while Attention+PCA means applying attention first then conduct dimensionality reduction with PCA. The results are shown in Fig. 4.

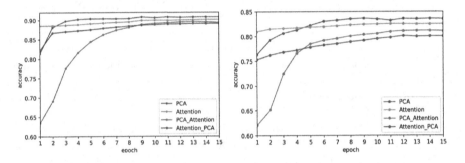

**Fig. 4.** Performance using different methods in feature fusion.

According to Fig. 4, it can be seen that PCA is superior to attention mechanism and other two combination methods in the feature fusion task. The possible reason is that the features extracted by each module are of equal importance, and hence attention mechanism does not work well in such case.

## 5   Conclusion

This paper proposes a fake news picture detection framework that combines multiple visual modalities and physical features. The proposed MVFNN consists of four main components: The visual modal module, the visual features fusion module, the physical features module and the ensemble module. The visual modal module is responsible for extracting image features from images pixel domain, frequency domain, and tamper detection. It cooperates with the visual features fusion module to detect fake news images from multi-vision fusion. The physical features module extract the physical feature such as the sharpness of images, and the ensemble module combines visual features and physical features to detect the fake news pictures. Experimental results show that our model could achieve better performance in benchmark datasets.

# References

1. Allcott, H., Gentzkow, M.: Social media and fake news in the 2016 election. J. Econ. Perspect. **31**(2), 211–36 (2017)
2. Shu, K., Sliva, A., Wang, S., Tang, J., Liu, H.: Fake news detection on social media: A data mining perspective. ACM SIGKDD Explor. Newsl. **19**(1), 22–36 (2017)
3. Kumar, S., Shah, N.: False information on web and social media: a survey. In: Social Media Analytics: Advances and Applications (2018)
4. Zubiaga, A., Aker, A., Bontcheva, K., Liakata, M., Procter, R.: Detection and resolution of rumours in social media: a survey. ACM Comput. Surv. (CSUR) **51**(2), 1–36 (2018)
5. Wu, L., Morstatter, F., Hu, X., Liu, H.: Mining misinformation in social media. In: Big Data in Complex and Social Networks, pp. 135–162. Chapman and Hall/CRC), UK (2016)
6. Jin, Z., Cao, J., Zhang, Y., Zhou, J., Tian, Q.: Novel visual and statistical image features for microblogs news verification. IEEE Trans. Multimedia **19**(3), 598–608 (2016)
7. Boididou, C., et al.: Verifying multimedia use at MediaEval 2015. MediaEval **3**(3), 7 (2015)
8. Wu, K., Yang, S., Zhu, K. Q.: False rumors detection on sina weibo by propagation structures. In: 2015 IEEE 31st International Conference on Data Engineering, South Korea, pp. 651–662. IEEE (2015)
9. Ma, J., Gao, W., Wong, K.F.: Detect rumors on Twitter by promoting information campaigns with generative adversarial learning. In: The World Wide Web Conference, USA, pp. 3049–3055. ACM (2019)
10. Shu, K., Wang, S., Liu, H.: Beyond news contents: the role of social context for fake news detection. In: Proceedings of the Twelfth ACM International Conference on Web Search and Data Mining, USA, pp. 312–320. ACM (2019)
11. Jin, Z., Cao, J., Guo, H., Zhang, Y., Luo, J.: Multimodal fusion with recurrent neural networks for rumor detection on microblogs. In: Proceedings of the 25th ACM international conference on Multimedia, USA, pp. 795–816. ACM (2017)
12. Wang, Y., Ma, F., Jin, Z., Yuan, Y., Xun, G., Jha, K., Gao, J.: Eann: Event adversarial neural networks for multi-modal fake news detection. In: Proceedings of the 24th acm sigkdd International Conference on Knowledge Discovery and Data Mining, UK, pp. 849–857. ACM (2018)
13. Khattar, D., Goud, J.S., Gupta, M., Varma, V.: Mvae: multimodal variational autoencoder for fake news detection. In: The World Wide Web Conference, USA, pp. 2915–2921. ACM (2019)
14. Qi, P., Cao, J., Yang, T., Guo, J., Li, J. : Exploiting multidomain visual information for fake news detection. In: 19th IEEE International Conference on Data Mining, China, IEEE (2019)
15. Masci, J., Meier, U., Cireşan, D., Schmidhuber, J.: Stacked convolutional auto-encoders for hierarchical feature extraction. In: Honkela, T., Duch, W., Girolami, M., Kaski, S. (eds.) ICANN 2011. LNCS, vol. 6791, pp. 52–59. Springer, Heidelberg (2011). https://doi.org/10.1007/978-3-642-21735-7_7
16. Yang, Y., Zheng, L., Zhang, J., Cui, Q., Li, Z., TI-CNN, P. Y. : Convolutional Neural Networks for Fake News Detection. arXiv preprint arXiv:1806.00749(2018)
17. Datasets1. https://biendata.com/competition/falsenews. Accessed 23 Oct 2019

# PEFS: A Validated Dataset for Perceptual Experiments on Face Swap Portrait Videos

Leslie Wöhler$^{(\boxtimes)}$ (iD), Jann-Ole Henningson$^{(\boxtimes)}$ (iD), Susana Castillo(iD),
and Marcus Magnor(iD)

Institut für Computergraphik, TU Braunschweig, Braunschweig, Germany
{Wohler,Henningson,Castillo,Magnor}@cg.cs.tu-bs.de
https://graphics.tu-bs.de/

**Abstract.** Videos obtained by current face swapping techniques can contain artifacts potentially detectable, yet unobtrusive to human observers. However, the perceptual differences between real and altered videos, as well as properties leading humans to classify a video as manipulated, are still unclear. Thus, to support the research on perceived realism and conveyed emotions in face swap videos, this paper introduces a high-resolution dataset providing the community with the necessary sophisticated stimuli.

Our recording process has been specifically designed to focus on human perception research and entails three scenarios (text-reading, emotion-triggering, and free-speech). We assess the perceived realness of our dataset through a series of experiments. The results indicate that our stimuli are overall convincing, even for long video sequences. Furthermore, we partially annotate the dataset with noticeable facial distortions and artifacts reported by participants.

**Keywords:** Video forensics · Video manipulation · Face swapping · Facial dataset · Human perception

## 1 Introduction

Current research has lead to a breakthrough in the editing process of video portraits enabling even the swapping of whole faces between actors with high quality and automation levels. With enough care, the quality of the obtained face swaps is high enough to be unobtrusive and, in some cases, even undetectable. However, there are still many open questions on how the perception of these manipulated videos differs from original videos, for example considering conveyed realism and emotions. Existing datasets of face swap videos were mainly designed to train and test automatic frameworks for manipulation detection [14,16,27]. While these offer a large number of manipulated video portraits, their lack of diversity in manipulation quality levels, displayed emotions, and playback durations limits their applicability to perceptual experiments.

---

L. Wöhler and J.-O. Henningson—Both authors contributed equally.

© Springer Nature Switzerland AG 2020
F. Tian et al. (Eds.): CASA 2020, CCIS 1300, pp. 120–127, 2020.
https://doi.org/10.1007/978-3-030-63426-1_13

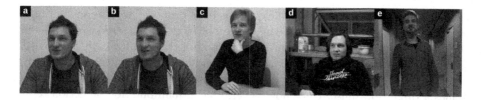

**Fig. 1.** Our dataset contains face swaps from controlled (a–c) and uncontrolled (d, e) environments using different camera angles and quality levels: (a) frontal view, (b) frontal with low manipulation quality, (c) wider view from the right side.

We introduce a new dataset of high-resolution face swaps specifically designed for perceptual experiments including recordings in controlled and uncontrolled environments with durations of up to 12 min (see Fig. 1). We first capture actors individually in front of a neutral white wall, while evoking a high variety of expressions by having actors read a text, participate in an interview, and show different emotions. Additionally, we include five uncontrolled sequences in different environments closer aligned to real world scenarios. We create three quality levels per face swap, allowing future experiments to further investigate the quality of manipulation as a factor, with its consequent associated artifacts and saliency. Our dataset is validated by perceptual experiments. We not only assess the perceived realism of different quality levels of stimuli, but also collect data on the saliency of facial areas and noticeable artifacts. Since we add these as annotations per stimulus, they can provide valuable insight towards which stimuli to select for perceptual experiments.

In summary, we contribute a novel dataset for Perceptual Experiments on Face Swaps (PEFS) which contains: *i)* All possibly derived face swap videos of up to 12 min length between 14 actors with 3 different quality levels and 3 camera angles captured in a homogeneous, controlled environment. We also include the corresponding real recordings totaling 630 videos; *ii)* A high variety of expressions induced via three different scenarios, including a free interview to evoke sincere emotions; *iii)* A set of uncontrolled sequences in real world environments featuring camera movements, varying lighting conditions, and occlusions; *iv)* Experimental validation and partial annotations on the perceived realism as well as the saliency of facial areas and notable artifacts aiding the stimuli selection for perceptual experiments.

## 2    Related Work

Recently, video manipulation techniques like face swapping have received a high interest from the research community leading to a fast development and improvement of facial manipulation approaches and datasets.

*Facial Manipulation and Detection.* Recent research on face swapping allows to easily switch the face of an actor with another person while keeping the original facial expressions [6,7,10]. In this field, it has been proposed to use convolutional neural networks along with the segmentation of faces [23], or adapting works in the field of style transfer [17]. In order to avoid full training for each source and target pair, Nirkin et al. introduced a face agnostic recurrent neural network [24]. Unfortunately, the availability and ease of use make facial manipulation techniques a target for abuse. Until now, several facial manipulation detection tools have been proposed, including approaches based on human physiology [11,19], temporal inconsistencies [12], or typical artifacts from neural networks [1,31].

*Facial Manipulation Datasets and Benchmarks.* Several datasets of face swap videos have been proposed focusing on different aspects like short clips of people reading out single sentences [17], realistic face swaps of celebrities [20], or a high amount of face swaps for training and evaluation of neural networks [8,14,26,27]. In contrast to these works, we aim to create a dataset specifically designed for perceptual research. Therefore, we record the original videos ourselves ensuring a high variance of actors and emotions as well as longer video duration while keeping a consistent environment. Additionally, we include different levels of manipulation quality and evoke various expressions.

*Perception of Faces and Emotions.* During social interactions, faces are essential for conveying emotions. Previous research shows that displayed emotions can influence viewing behaviour and that participants tend to focus on specific facial regions when processing the displayed emotions [4,9,18]. However, there are a variety of factors influencing our viewing behaviour, e.g. cultural background [5,25], familiarity with other people [2,30], gender [22,29], or even artifacts [3]. Considering all these very specialised responses to human faces – and even when face swaps, generally, aim to preserve the conveyed information and emotion of the original actor – poses the question of how the perception of state-of-the-art face swaps differs from real videos. Thus, we carefully design our dataset to help investigating these differences by providing homogeneous, high-quality face swaps of various actors.

## 3   Dataset

Capturing the videos in a **controlled environment** allows us to explicitly choose a script for the recordings and obtain different expressions from each actor. Additionally, we restrict the lighting conditions and movement range of actors. This way, we can produce high-quality face swaps with a variety of facial expressions while reducing external distractions. Our recording setup is shown in Fig. 2 (left). In this setup, the actor sits at a table in front of a white wall. There are no other items in the scene as to not distract from the actor.

Naturally, people are akin to looking straight forward instead of sideways [28], leading to an unequal distribution of facial positions inside the recordings. In order to increase the variety of stimuli and obtain stimuli with and without eye-contact, we simultaneously record from three angles shown in Fig. 2. Similar

**Fig. 2.** Setup of the recordings in the controlled environment and snapshots of the recording of an actor from the three different camera angles

to forward-looking facial positions, neutral facial expressions are more probable than non-neutral expressions, leading to an unchangeable bias inside the data in that regard. To include a high variety of expressions, we split the recording in three parts. First the actors had to read a short text twice. This offers us a short sequence with minimal movements allowing for a neutral condition which can also be generated in very high quality. In the second part, we induced 11 different emotions (Agreement, Disagreement, Cluelessness, Thinking, Pain, Happiness, Sadness, Anger, Disgust, Fear and Surprise) based on a method acting protocol [15]. The third and last part consisted of free-talking in which the examiner asked the actor different questions. To guarantee the existence of different facial positions in the third part, the conductor of the recordings made sure to stay in the center of gaze and guided the view by walking around the room.

We also include recordings in **uncontrolled environments** into our dataset, as these have a closer resemblance to many real-world scenarios. To maximize the heterogeneity in this part of the dataset, recordings were made in several varying lighting conditions, environments and used different camera parameters. We recorded a set of five different scenes including actions like walking down a hallway or eating snacks. Each action was performed by at least two actors. We recorded the scenes from different distances, e.g. full-body views, close-ups or angles depicting the actor from the hip up. Moreover, some videos contain dynamic movement of the actor and camera alike as well as minor and major occlusions.

In total, we recorded 14 actors (3 female, 11 male) of an average age of 25. We gathered 42 controlled videos, all recorded with a resolution of 1920 times 1080 pixels and durations between 9 and 12 min. Additionally, we recorded 10 videos of 3 min each in uncontrolled environments of 3 males ($age \approx 24$).

We use DeepFaceLab [6] to produce face swaps between all actors and stop training after 25, 50 and 100 thousand epochs to create three quality levels per video.

## 4    Perceptual Validation

We conducted two experiments (E1 and E2) to evaluate and annotate our dataset. In these experiments, we asses the perceived realism along with notable artifacts for high and low-quality face swaps in the controlled environment. Both experiments follow the same design and only differ in the selected stimuli. The first experiment, E1, uses high-quality face swaps generated after 100 thousand epochs of training (SwapHQ), while the second experiment, E2, uses the same videos in lower quality, generated after 25 thousand epochs (SwapLQ). In the experiments, we also included the original video (Real) of the actor for each manipulated video. Participants either saw the real or the manipulated version of each video. Note that the quality of the real videos is the same in E1 and E2. We manually selected 11 representative face swaps from our dataset using 2 female-to-female and 7 male-to-male swaps. Additionally, we included 2 face swaps of mixed genders (a female face on a male body and vice-versa). For each of these videos, we chose a 60 s clip so that the chosen stimuli include different movements and expressions. This duration gives the viewer enough time to fully explore the scene and can contain diverse facial expressions.

The experiment proceeded as follows. First, the participant was given an explanation on the concept of face swapping and was introduced to the task of detecting face swap videos. Each trial started with the automatic playback of a video. The participant was not able to stop, pause or replay the stimulus. Once the video finished, it was replaced with a screen displaying the question for the first task (2AFC): 'Was this video manipulated?' and two possible answers: *Real* or *Manipulated*. The participant had to select one of them in order to continue the experiment. Then, the screen displayed the question for the second – in this case non-forced-multiple-choice (NFMC) – task: "Which facial areas were most important for your decision?" together with the following list of possible answers (Eyes, Eyebrows, Contour, Cheeks, Nose, Mouth, None of Above). If the video was reported as a face swap, an additional question about notable artifacts – also in the form of a NFMC task – was presented (Blur, Overlapping Contours, Unnatural Facial Expressions, Irregular Skin Color, Deformed Facial Features, Beauty Filter Effect, None of the Above). This process was repeated until the participant saw all 11 stimuli (in a random order with different order per participant). The average time for each participant to complete the experiment was of 15 min. We conducted both experiments using Amazon Mechanical Turk. A total of 24 participants took part in E1 and 20 in E2. They were compensated with 1 Euro and could only take part in one of the experiments.

Based on the experiments, we analyse our dataset with regard to the perceived realism and notable artifacts.

*Perceived Realism.* We first analyse the assessment accuracy of both experiments as shown in Fig. 3. We find that participants believed around 65% of the high-quality face swaps and 50% of the low-quality face swaps to be real videos. As a baseline, we include the accuracy for the corresponding real stimuli, which was around 80% in both E1 and E2. Therefore, our high-quality face swaps were overall very convincing, even though they still cannot reach the same level as real videos. This is especially interesting as it indicates that our face swaps can keep a high quality even for a rather long duration of 60 s. Even though our low-quality face swaps are easier to distinguish from real videos, they are still

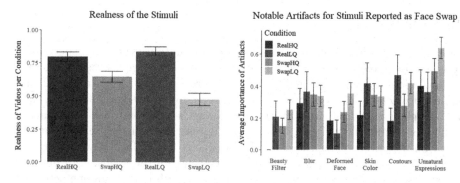

**Fig. 3.** Left: perceived realness for each condition. Participants perceived around 65% of our high-quality face swaps and 50% of our low-quality face swaps as real. Right: Reported importance of artifacts for each condition when labelling a video as a face swap. Error bars represent the standard error of the mean (SEM).

not fully unconvincing. Therefore, they can be valuable for experiments as a stimulus variation with stronger artifacts or for comparative purposes.

*Important Facial Areas and Notable Artifacts.* Next to the perceived realism, we also looked into which facial areas are most important for the decision of participants. In Fig. 4 the left plot shows which facial areas were selected by participants when deciding a stimulus was a real video, the right plot shows results for stimuli reported to be face swaps. For both cases, the mouth, the nose and the eye region are most important for the decision of participants. This is in line with previous research that finds these are the most important areas for facial recognition [13,21]. Looking into the notable artifacts presented in Fig. 4, we see that participants especially noticed unnatural expressions, inconsistent skin color and a beauty filter effect. Additionally, stimuli in E2 were often reported to contain overlapping contours.

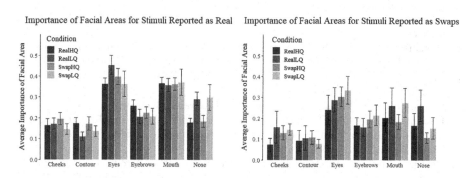

**Fig. 4.** Reported importance of facial regions when labelling a video as real (left) or as face swap (right). Error bars indicate the SEM.

# 5   Conclusion

We presented PEFS: A novel dataset of high-resolution face swaps specifically designed for perceptual research. In contrast to previous datasets, we include manipulations of different quality levels, recording duration of up to 12 min, anonymous actors, and a high variation of expressions. Our dataset offers a total of 14 original recordings from three camera angles in a controlled environment yielding a total of 630 videos. Finally, our dataset is evaluated and annotated based on perceived realism and notable artifacts. In the future, we would like to further expand the dataset. Possible extensions are the inclusion of outdoor scenes in natural lighting conditions or sequences with more than one actor.

**Acknowledgments.** The authors gratefully acknowledge funding by the German Science Foundation (DFG MA2555/15-1 "Immersive Digital Reality"), and the L3S Research Center, Hanover, Germany.

# References

1. Afchar, D., Nozick, V., Yamagishi, J., Echizen, I.: Mesonet: a compact facial video forgery detection network. In: 2018 IEEE International Workshop on Information Forensics and Security (WIFS), pp. 1–7. IEEE (2018)
2. Althoff, R., Cohen, N.: Eye-movement-based memory effect: a reprocessing effect in face perception. J. Exp. Psychol. Learn. Mem. Cogn. **25**(4), 997–1010 (1999)
3. Bombari, D., Mast, F.W., Lobmaier, J.S.: Featural, configural, and holistic face-processing strategies evoke different scan patterns. Perception **38**(10), 1508–1521 (2009)
4. Calvo, M.G., Nummenmaa, L.: Eye-movement assessment of the time course in facial expression recognition: neurophysiological implications. Cogn. Affect. Behav. Neurosci. **9**(4), 398–411 (2009). https://doi.org/10.3758/CABN.9.4.398
5. Chua, H., Boland, J., Nisbett, R.: Cultural variation in eye movement during scene perception. Proc. Natl. Acad. Sci. USA **102**, 12629–33 (2005)
6. Deepfacelab (2019). https://github.com/iperov/DeepFaceLab
7. Deepfakes face manipulation framework (2019). https://github.com/deepfakes/faceswap
8. Dolhansky, B., Howes, R., Pflaum, B., Baram, N., Ferrer, C.C.: The deepfake detection challenge (DFDC) preview dataset. arXiv preprint arXiv:1910.08854 (2019)
9. Eisenbarth, H., Alpers, G.W.: Happy mouth and sad eyes: scanning emotional facial expressions. Emotion **11**(4), 860 (2011)
10. Faceswap (2019). https://github.com/MarekKowalski/FaceSwap
11. Fernandes, S., et al.: Predicting heart rate variations of deepfake videos using neural ode. In: Proceedings of the IEEE International Conference on Computer Vision Workshops (2019)
12. Güera, D., Delp, E.J.: Deepfake video detection using recurrent neural networks. In: 2018 15th IEEE International Conference on Advanced Video and Signal Based Surveillance (AVSS), pp. 1–6. IEEE (2018)
13. Janik, S.W., Wellens, A.R., Goldberg, M.L., Dell'Osso, L.F.: Eyes as the center of focus in the visual examination of human faces. Percept. Mot. Skills **47**(3), 857–858 (1978)

14. Jiang, L., Li, R., Wu, W., Qian, C., Loy, C.C.: Deeperforensics-1.0: a large-scale dataset for real-world face forgery detection. In: The IEEE/CVF Conference on Computer Vision and Pattern Recognition (CVPR) (2020)
15. Kaulard, K., Cunningham, D.W., Bülthoff, H.H., Wallraven, C.: The MPI facial expression database - a validated database of emotional and conversational facial expressions. PLoS ONE **7**(3), e32321 (2012)
16. Korshunov, P., Marcel, S.: Vulnerability assessment and detection of Deepfake videos. In: 2019 International Conference on Biometrics (ICB), pp. 1–6 (2019)
17. Korshunova, I., Shi, W., Dambre, J., Theis, L.: Fast face-swap using convolutional neural networks. In: Proceedings of the IEEE International Conference on Computer Vision, pp. 3677–3685 (2017)
18. Wells, L.J., Gillespie, S.M., Rotshtein, P.: Identification of emotional facial expressions: effects of expression, intensity, and sex on eye gaze. PLoS ONE **11**(12), 0168307 (2016)
19. Li, Y., Chang, M.C., Lyu, S.: In ictu oculi: Exposing AI created fake videos by detecting eye blinking. In: IEEE International Workshop on Information Forensics and Security (WIFS), pp. 1–7 (2018)
20. Li, Y., Yang, X., Sun, P., Qi, H., Lyu, S.: Celeb-DF: a large-scale challenging dataset for deepfake forensics. In: Proceedings of the IEEE/CVF Conference on Computer Vision and Pattern Recognition (CVPR), pp. 3207–3216 (2020)
21. Mertens, I., Siegmund, H., Grüsser, O.J.: Gaze motor asymmetries in the perception of faces during a memory task. Neuropsychologia **31**(9), 989–998 (1993)
22. Murray, I.J., Parry, N.R.A., McKeefry, D.J., Panorgias, A.: Sex-related differences in peripheral human color vision: a color matching study. J. Vis. **12**(1), 18–18 (2012)
23. Nirkin, Y., Keller, Y., Hassner, T.: FSGAN: Subject agnostic face swapping and reenactment. In: ICCV (2019)
24. Nirkin, Y., Masi, I., Tuan, A.T., Hassner, T., Medioni, G.: On face segmentation, face swapping, and face perception. In: 13th IEEE International Conference on Automatic Face & Gesture Recognition, pp. 98–105 (2018)
25. Nisbett, R.E.: The geography of thought: how asians and... westerners think differently and why. Free Press, New York (2003)
26. Rössler, A., Cozzolino, D., Verdoliva, L., Riess, C., Thies, J., Nießner, M.: Faceforensics: a large-scale video dataset for forgery detection in human faces. CoRR abs/1803.09179 (2018)
27. Rössler, A., Cozzolino, D., Verdoliva, L., Riess, C., Thies, J., Nießner, M.: Faceforensics++: learning to detect manipulated facial images. In: ICCV 2019 (2019)
28. Rönnqvist, L., Hopkins, B.: Head position preference in the human newborn: a new look. Child Dev. **69**(1), 13–23 (1998)
29. Shaqiri, A., et al.: Sex-related differences in vision are heterogeneous. Sci. Rep. **8**(7521), 1–10 (2018)
30. Van Belle, G., Ramon, M., Lefèvre, P., Rossion, B.: Fixation patterns during recognition of personally familiar and unfamiliar faces. Front. Psychol. **1**, 20 (2010)
31. Wang, S.Y., Wang, O., Zhang, R., Owens, A., Efros, A.A.: CNN-generated images are surprisingly easy to spot... for now. arXiv preprint arXiv:1912.11035 (2019)

# Altering the Conveyed Facial Emotion Through Automatic Reenactment of Video Portraits

Colin Groth[✉][iD], Jan-Philipp Tauscher[iD], Susana Castillo[iD], and Marcus Magnor[iD]

Institut für Computergraphik, TU Braunschweig, Braunschweig, Germany
{Groth,Tauscher,Castillo,Magnor}@cg.cs.tu-bs.de
https://graphics.tu-bs.de/

**Abstract.** Current facial reenactment techniques are able to generate results with a high level of photo-realism and temporal consistency. Although the technical possibilities are rapidly progressing, recent techniques focus on achieving fast, visually plausible results. Further perceptual effects caused by altering the original facial expressivity of the recorded individual are disregarded. By investigating the influence of altered facial movements on the perception of expressions we aim to generate not only physically possible but truly believable reenactments.

In this paper we perform two experiments using a modified state-of-the-art technique to reenact a video portrait of a person with different expressions gathered from a validated database of motion captured facial expressions to better understand the impact of reenactments.

**Keywords:** Facial reenactment · Video manipulation · Facial expressions · Perception

## 1 Introduction and Related Work

Manipulating facial movements in images and videos in a photo-realistic way has become possible with recent advances in computer graphics. These techniques can be used to alter expressions as needed, sometimes even in real-time and usually with a neural network at their core. In particular, Generative Adversarial Networks (GANs) [8] and Auto-Regressive Networks [13] are a frequently used tool to synthesise high quality images. Facial reenactment is usually done by using depth information besides the RGB video input [9,18], or a parametric model [6]. Less restrictive was the seminal approach of Thies et al., capable of reenacting common RGB videos in real-time [16]. The authors used a markerless face tracker for face detection without any additional depth information. Although the synthesis of videos is possible at a high quality rate, producing temporally-consistent synthesised videos is a challenging problem that has a long research trajectory. One example for an approach that made the video-to-video synthesis more temporally-consistent is the work of Wang et al. [17]. With

F. Tian et al. (Eds.): CASA 2020, CCIS 1300, pp. 128–135, 2020.
https://doi.org/10.1007/978-3-030-63426-1_14

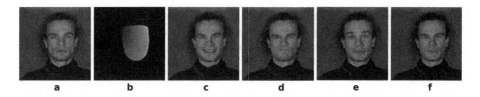

**Fig. 1.** This paper uses a modified state-of-the-art technique that operates on the *uv* maps (b) of the manipulated meshes. We alter the facial expression of an input video (a) to display happiness (c), disbelief (d), positive surprise (e) and disgust (f).

their vid2vid framework they were able to produce high-resolution, temporally-consistent video results. Their approach uses a conditional GAN for short-term temporal coherence. Despite the positive characteristics of the vid2vid approach, it is not directly related to faces. A further improvement in facial reenactment in terms of quality was done by Thies et al. with the Deferred Neural Rendering method [15]. This technique allows to use imperfect face meshes and still generate a high quality photo-realistic reenactment. For this, the authors use a neural renderer to interpret the object-specific Neural Textures.

All methods of facial reenactment mentioned above focus mainly on the technical implementation rather than on the correct perception of affective meaning. However, the community is aware of the importance, as it can trigger the uncanny valley effect [11] on the viewer in line with the recent work of Mittal et al. [14]. Thus, a method able to generate emotions that convey the desired meaning while keeping the original look of the person in a photo-realistic manner would have great advantages. Furthermore, given that no human is good (or even capable), to perform all possible facial expressions, as shown in previous research [3,4], such a tool could help overcome this deficit since the emotions could be subsequently adjusted.

In this paper, we focus on a post-processing alternative that exploits the great potential of automatically generated facial reenactments to be an effective and efficient tool to improve quality and comprehensibility of videos, making re-shots dispensable in such situations. We modified a state-of-the-art tool capable of reenacting facial expression in video portraits, by adapting it to be able to use motion capture (MoCap) data as source input instead of videos. To the best of our knowledge, this is the first reenacting technique that uses MoCap data as a basis for the manipulation of facial expressions. The presented tool allows us to easily reenact facial emotions on user-provided videos with motion captured facial expressions. In the pursuit of the long-term goal of generating novel expressions from existing data, MoCap data provides the genuine advantage of providing precise 3D representations that can be used for multidimensional operations like interpolation between expressions.

Based on the reenacted videos resulting from our technique, we gathered empirical data on how reenacted emotions are perceived. Our experiment studies the perception of Recognition, Intensity and Sincerity (RIS) of the reenacted facial emotions with a focus on the conveyed and intended meaning. The results demonstrate how reliably specific emotions can be generated and how they will appear to the viewer, especially in comparison with the real videos of the same emotions.

## 2  Reenacting Technique

Reenactments describe the rendering of images or videos from a new perspective or manipulated aspect. In this work we investigate the generation of photo-realistic renderings of video portraits by MoCap data with a focus on the representation of the emotional state.

This work uses face tracking based on facial landmark detection to gather the required information about key point positions in the video portraits. The tracking that is used to find the face position in the video frames is done by the open-source library Dlib [10]. Since the tracking itself is image-based and, therefore, time independent, it often contains high-frequency noise. To stabilize the face tracking over time an exponential moving average filter is applied on the detected face positions. This filtering technique was used because it is efficient and can be applied on the data in place. A 3D mask model of the face is gained by reconstructing it joint-based by a Position Map Regression Network (PRN) [7]. Furthermore, the dense alignment and an estimation of the head pose relative to the camera position results from the PRN method. The 3D facial mesh provides the foundation for the facial reenactment process.

Our approach focuses on the use of MoCap data as a basis for facial reenactments instead of using videos. MoCap data has the decisive advantage that it is represented in three dimensions. The benefit of having 3D data is that multiple operations can be done much easier, like interpolating between different emotions to generate movement data for emotions that are not captured at all. Such an interpolation for 2D video inputs would require to generate 3D face representations out of the videos, as expressions are 3D. This dimensional upscaling is still part of current research and not focus of this work. For the emotion based mesh manipulation, we use the facial expressions MoCap database created by Castillo et al. [2]. This dataset fits our purpose because it contains natural emotions of which the recognizability has already been validated [2,3]. In addition, we use a second dataset that was captured by us. It contains video portraits of twelve different emotions from the target person that is to be reenacted.

The facial manipulation procedure applied in this work uses the face mesh and the MoCap data as input. In order to know how much each of the 62 MoCap markers influences all of the vertices of the full face mesh we calculate the corresponding weights in a pre-process step by the quadratic distance between the MoCap markers and the particular vertices. The quadratic distance is used as it results in the most accurate emotional representations based on visual investigation. As both datasets, the face mesh and the MoCap datapoints, are defined in their own spaces, for every frame they are merged into a uniform 3D space before transformation. Note, that the head motion is removed from the source data, as our current focus is only on facial movements. The final reenacted face motions result from a weighted combination of the MoCap data and the expressions of the target person extracted from video footage, as follows:

$$M_{final} = w_1 * M_{mocap} + w_2 * M_{target},$$ (1)

with weights $w_1 + w_2 = 1$. $M$ represents the matrix of the $n$ 3D vertices. Before the face mesh movements of the target person are used in Eq. 1 we applied a median filter with a five frames kernel to mitigate the impact of movement noise from imperfect tracking and reconstruction.

Finally, to render the final reenacted videos, we employ deferred neural rendering [15]. This method is used in our work as it allows to produce photo-realistic renderings from imperfect 3D meshes. As inputs for the rendering network, pairs of $uv$ maps and their corresponding images are used (see Fig. 1).

## 3    Experimental Design

We used a standardized RIS framework with forced-choice tasks to examine how reenactment modulates the perception of the expressivity of an individual. We considered two different conditions, both with a different group of participants. In the first condition (C1) participants were only exposed to the real videos ($_{rv}$) of both actors – the target actor ($JPT$) and the MoCap actor ($CJC$) – showing the chosen emotions, while in the second condition (C2) the reenacted videos ($_{re}$) of the same chosen emotions were used as stimuli.

*Stimuli.* Two datasets were used for the generation of the stimuli displayed in both experiments. The first dataset was the MoCap dataset with the corresponding real videos as described in Sect. 2 while the second consisted of video portraits of the target person. We selected four representative emotions (two positive and two negative) from both datasets: *happiness, positive surprise, disbelief* and *disgust.* These emotions were selected for being easily recognizable even in the absence of head motion [4,12]. Additionally, a neutral video of the target person was used as basis for the reenactments. This video shows the person with neutral or dimmed expressions while talking in a quite still position.

The second condition (C2) included three different types of reenactments, differing in their representation of the weighted combination of $w_1$ and $w_2$ from Eq. 1: *1)* $w_1 = 0$ and $w_2 = 1$ ($JPT_{re}$). These expressions are only based on the facial movement of the target person. They are to show how stable the render method is and how much noise is introduced by using MoCap. *2)* $w_1 = 1$ and $w_2 = 0$ ($MOCAP_{re}$). The expressions in these videos are fully based on the MoCap data and demonstrate how good emotions are recognised when they are transferred from MoCap. *3)* $w_1 = 0.5$ and $w_2 = 0.5$ ($Mix_{re}$). These expressions consist of the movement of the target person and the MoCap data equally and will allow a comparison of the two sources.

All reenacted videos as well as the real videos were displayed from and to neutral expression when showing an emotion. The length of the videos varied between two and five seconds and all were post-processed to $720 \times 720$ px at 50 fps.

*Procedure.* Both conditions followed the same procedure, controlled by Psychophysics Toolbox Version 3.0.11 (PTB-3) [1]. After fulfilling an informed consent and collecting demographic data, each participant sat, one at a time, in the experiment room in front of a 24-in. screen ($1920 \times 1080$ px, 60 Hz). The concepts of RIS were explained on screen at the beginning of the experiment. During a trial, participants watched the videos of the four emotions (*happiness*, *positive surprise*, *disbelief* and *disgust*) for every actor. The presentation of the stimuli followed a blockwise design by type of reenactment. Within a type, the order of presentation of the emotions was fully randomized, with each participant being assigned a different order. For all videos, no repetitions were possible to force the viewers to decide by their first impression. For every video, the participants were asked to answer three multiple-choice questions: "Which emotion is expressed?", "How intense is the emotion expressed?", and "How sincere is the emotion expressed?". While the first question was categorical (forced choice), the other two were asked to be rated on a seven-point Likert-scale going from 1 "extremely low" to 7 "extremely high". After finishing all tasks the results were checked for completeness and the participants were compensated with 10€ or equal internal university's course credit. The average time to complete the experiment was 11 min 42 s.

A total of 21 participants (11 females, age 18–32, mean 24.1, SD 3.05) completed the real videos condition (C1), while 22 people (10 females, 19–57, mean 26.45, SD 11.01) participated in the experiment for the reenacted videos condition (C2).

## 4    Results and Discussion

The results of the experiment for both conditions are illustrated in Fig. 2. The results of the three types of reenactments (C2) are shown side by side with those of the real videos (C1) for better visualization. For the analysis of the experimental results, a two-way ANOVA per averaged dimension –with type of reenactment and emotion as within-participant factors– was done for each of the two conditions.

The condition for the reenacted videos (C2) showed a significant effect on the emotion for the **Recognition**, $F(3, 336) = 16.5, p < 0.001$. In comparison, for the condition with the real videos (C1) there was no significant effect on the emotion. All these results were independent from the technique used. From these results it can be concluded that the type of an emotion displayed in a reenacted video matters in terms of recognizability. In this experiment, participants had no problem identifying the emotions from the real videos following the average recognition rates of over 80%. The results from the reenactments of C2 show comparable ratings. All emotions were well recognised except for *disgust*. The recognition rates of *disgust* are only around chance level for all reenactment

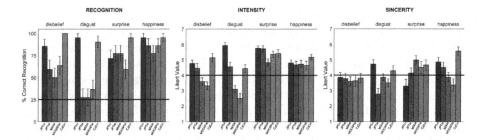

**Fig. 2.** Ratings for the reenacted videos (C2: $JPT_{re}, MIX_{re}, MOCAP_{re}$) anchored by the results from the original videos (C1: $JPT_{rv}, CJC_{rv}$). In reading order: recognition rates per expression and type of video; ratings for their perceived intensity; and ratings for perceived sincerity. Error bars represent the standard error of the mean, the chance line is drawn in black.

styles suggesting that participants were not able to detect this emotion. In particular, positive emotions were better identified than negative ones, based on the recognition rates, what also confirms previous research findings [3,5]. The rates of *positive surprise* even surpassed the results of the ground truth results of the target actor $(JPT_{rv})$.

A closer look showed that in those scenarios where the judgements of the participants were not accurate regarding recognition, it took the participants about ten times longer to vote, indicating their insecurity about their judgements. *Disgust* was not generally mistaken for another emotion, but the rates are for the most part evenly distributed among the possible answers. These results indicate that the participants generally did not mistake this emotion for another, but guessed it instead. Only for the reenactments with movements of the MoCap actor $(MOCAP_{re}$ and $Mix_{re})$ a trend of the wrong answers toward *disbelief* occurred (50.0% of the ratings) that supports the confusion between the two negative emotions, which also appeared in the classification of *disbelief* itself (around 40% mistaken for *disgust*). A possible reason for the bad recognition of *disgust* might be that it involves more than only facial motion and needs additional information to be recognised. As other motions were not reenacted in the videos the required information for recognition of the emotion may have been lost.

The experiment also suggests that the **Intensity** of the conveyed emotion can be altered. The results of the experiment show a significant effect for the reenactments (C2) for both style and emotion, all $F's > 26.25$, all $p's < 0.001$. For the real videos of C1 an effect was also present for emotions $(F(3, 160) = 3.16, p < 0.02)$. In contrast to recognition, the reenactment technique has an influence here. The intensities of the emotions from the real videos were all ranked above the average "neutral" value (score 4) on the Likert scale. Comparing this to the C2 ratings, it can be seen that the assessments made for *positive surprise* and *happiness* are almost identical to their comparatives. This indicates that positive emotions can be transferred effectively through reenactment. For the emotion *disgust* the ratings are quite low. This is not surprising considering that this emotion was not recognised reliably. The ratings for *disbelief* show a clear distinction between the different styles. For the reenactment done by the full input of the target actor (scale $JPT_{re}$) the intensity ratings are comparable to the ones of the real videos of the same person. In contrast, the reenactments fully resulting from the MoCap data differ from its comparative rating by the real videos. This deviation indicates that the MoCap data of this expression alters the intensity of the real emotion. This finding is reinforced by the fact that the rating of the intensity of the equal weight combination (namely $Mix_{re}$) of both styles lies between both. This distribution between the different movement weightings is apparent for almost all emotions and shows the clear possibility that the intensity can be altered by the percentage of MoCap movements used.

For the **Sincerity** of the emotions, the experiment indicates that a manipulation by reenacting a video is not possible. For both conditions, the experiment results demonstrate a significant effect of emotion for the sincerity of expression, $F(3, 160) = 7.52, p < 0.001$ (C1) and $F(3, 336) = 7.39, p < 0.001$ (C2). However, no effect of style could be detected. The analytical results clearly reveal that the sincerity of an emotion is not affected by the performed reenactment. This means that the sincerity of facial movements does not get lost when manipulating a video by reenactment. This result presents a positive perspective for the use of reenactments to create believable result videos. In other words, an emotional expression may not be made more authentic by reenactment. Nevertheless, it must be noted that this result depends heavily on the emotion chosen. For *disbelief* and *positive surprise* a well balanced distribution can be seen which is aligned to the values of the real videos. For the other two dimensions, however, the results are not aligned with the real videos, even though they are evenly distributed over the different movement proportions of the reenactments.

## 5   Conclusion

In this paper, we probed into the meaning of facial emotions when the movement is altered. The input videos were reenacted using our tool which combines different facial movements including MoCap data to create the desired expressions. Despite the existing future opportunities, we believe this work provides significant insights into the perception of emotions and their possible manipulation through facial reenactment.

Our experimental results indicate that reenacted videos are able to manipulate the conveyed facial emotions by generating expressions that are recognised correctly, i.e., the movements of one person can be mapped onto another and still preserve the conveyed meaning. Furthermore, we also showed that, while video reenactment is also able to alter the intensity of the conveyed emotion, it cannot deliberately change its sincerity.

**Acknowledgments.** The authors gratefully acknowledge funding by the German Science Foundation (DFG MA2555/15-1 "Immersive Digital Reality").

# References

1. Brainard, D.H.: The psychophysics toolbox. Spat. Vis. **10**, 433–436 (1997)
2. Castillo, S., Legde, K., Cunningham, D.W.: The semantic space for motion-captured facial expressions. Comput. Animation Virtual Worlds **29**(3–4), e1823 (2018)
3. Castillo, S., Wallraven, C., Cunningham, D.W.: The semantic space for facial communication. Comput. Animation Virtual Worlds **25**(3–4), 223–231 (2014)
4. Cunningham, D.W., Kleiner, M., Wallraven, C., Bülthoff, H.H.: Manipulating video sequences to determine the components of conversational facial expressions. ACM Trans. Appl. Percept. **2**(3), 251–269 (2005)
5. Cunningham, D.W., Wallraven, C.: The interaction between motion and form in expression recognition. In: Proceedings of the ACM Symposium on Applied Perception in Graphics and Visualization, pp. 41–44 (2009)
6. Dale, K., Sunkavalli, K., Johnson, M.K., Vlasic, D., Matusik, W., Pfister, H.: Video face replacement. ACM Trans. Graph. **30**(6), 1–10 (2011)
7. Feng, Y., Wu, F., Shao, X., Wang, Y., Zhou, X.: Joint 3D face reconstruction and dense alignment with position map regression network. In: European Conference on Computer Vision (2018)
8. Goodfellow, I., et al.: Generative adversarial nets. In: Advances in Neural Information Processing Systems, pp. 2672–2680 (2014)
9. Kemelmacher-Shlizerman, I., Sankar, A., Shechtman, E., Seitz, S.M.: Being john malkovich. In: European Conference on Computer Vision, pp. 341–353 (2010)
10. King, D.E.: Dlib-ml: A machine learning toolkit. J. Mach. Learn. Res. **10**, 1755–1758 (2009). http://www.dlib.net
11. Mori, M., MacDorman, K., Kageki, N.: The uncanny valley. IEEE Robot Autom. Mag. **19**(2), 98–100 (2012)
12. Nusseck, M., Cunningham, D.W., Wallraven, C., Bülthoff, H.H.: The contribution of different facial regions to the recognition of conversational expressions. J. Vis. **8**(8), 1–23 (2008)
13. Van den Oord, A., Kalchbrenner, N., Espeholt, L., Vinyals, O., Graves, A., Kavukcuoglu, K.: Conditional image generation with PixelCNN decoders. In: Advances in Neural Information Processing Systems, pp. 4790–4798 (2016)
14. Mittal, T., Bhattacharya, U., Chandra, R., et al.: Emotions don't lie: A deepfake detection method using audio-visual affective cues (2020). arXiv:2003.06711
15. Thies, J., Zollhöfer, M., Nießner, M.: Deferred neural rendering: Image synthesis using neural textures. ACM Trans. Graph. **38**(4), 66:1–66:12 (2019)
16. Thies, J., Zollhöfer, M., Stamminger, M., Theobalt, C., Nießner, M.: Face2face: real-time face capture and reenactment of RGB videos. In: Proceedings of the IEEE Conference on Computer Vision and Pattern Recognition, pp. 2387–2395 (2016)
17. Wang, T.C., et al.: Video-to-video synthesis. In: Advances in Neural Information Processing Systems (2018)
18. Weise, T., Bouaziz, S., Li, H., Pauly, M.: Realtime performance-based facial animation. ACM Trans. Graph. **30**(4), 1–10 (2011)

# Author Index

Printed in the United States
By Bookmasters